John T. Humphrey

Understanding and Using Baptismal Records

Humphrey Publications
1996

UNDERSTANDING AND USING BAPTISMAL RECORDS

COVER ILLUSTRATION: "Baptism of Virginia Dare"
(courtesy of the Prints and Photographs Division, Library of Congress)

Library of Congress Catalog Card No. 95–95327
ISBN: 1–887609–10–5

Camera-ready copy prepared by Publishing Plus, Yardley, Pennsylvania.
Printed in the United States of America.

For further information or additional copies, please contact:

John T. Humphrey
P.O. Box 15190
Washington, DC 20003

To Larry

With appreciation and special thanks to Marion Frack Egge, editor of the *Pennsylvania Genealogical Magazine*, for her encouragement, helpful suggestions, and technical expertise.

Contents

Charts and Illustrations

Charts and Illustrations

Chapter 1

Introduction to the Issues

Everyone engaged in tracing a modern American family history into the late seventeenth and early eighteenth centuries—beginners and professional genealogists alike—will, at some point, face the issues of baptismal records. Just as detectives are obligated to track down and verify all possible clues, however apparently irrelevant to a case, so also must the family historian be willing to travel roads that may lead nowhere.

A family historian cannot assume, once an ancestor's religious affiliation and place of residence have been documented, that the baptisms of children born into the family were actually performed or recorded—and, if so, when and where. Some early churches, in Colonial days as well as today, practiced adult baptism; one faith, the Religious Society of Friends, rejected baptism entirely. Then as now, families tied to non-baptizing religious denominations sometimes followed customs outside the dictates of their own church leaders. Furthermore, it is not uncommon for people to accept new religious principles following an inter-denominational marriage. For example, a staunchly dedicated Catholic family during the nineteenth and twentieth centuries may not always have belonged to the Catholic Church or may not always have strictly followed Catholic doctrine. The same would hold true for members of other religious faiths.

Astute researchers in any discipline take the time to look beyond the obvious; the exploration of seemingly obscure areas can sometimes yield surprising results. Learning as much as possible about comparative baptismal practice can prove to be one of the basic reference points for genealogists. Both the knowledge of and the application of basic theological principles as presented in this text—those relating specifically to a variety of baptismal traditions within a historical context encompassing the periods from the birth of Judeo-Christian religion into and throughout the eighteenth-century migration of settlers from Europe to the New World—are essential to scholarly genealogical research. Having this information at one's fingertips provides insight into not only the actual keeping of baptismal records in Colonial Pennsylvania, but also into some of the reasons why some records are extant and others are not.

In using the principles presented in this book, genealogists should be aware of several potential stumbling blocks resulting from changes in terminology over the past several centuries. The "Anglican Church" of today is called the "Protestant Episcopal Church" in the United States; the "Dunkards" are now known as members of the "Church of the Brethren"; the "Methodist Church" simply added a prefix to become the "United Methodist Church"; the "German Reformed Church" underwent a radical name change, becoming the "United Church of Christ." Researchers should remember, too, that the names of many churches may have been altered since their founding dates through mergers or other circumstances.

While this book focuses on the prevailing religious groups and early baptismal records within an early Pennsylvania setting, it also provides the background of theology and ritual representing practitioners of all faiths—Church of England, Presbyterian, Catholic, Lutheran, etc.—without regard to residence, be it Pennsylvania, Virginia, or Massachusetts. The theology and background for each religion—as well as the living conditions—were pretty much the same in all locations. It should, therefore, not come as a surprise that many of the common problems encountered by genealogists working with Pennsylvania records are virtually duplicated within baptismal registers found in any or all of the original thirteen colonies.

In addition to learning about the theological foundations that influenced baptismal practice and record-keeping, researchers must keep in mind that certain environmental, political, and social factors contributed to the conditions under which early Colonial records were kept and are available today. Difficult as it may seem, present-day genealogists must be able to recognize a reality different from the one experienced today—a period when the primary form of communication was direct verbal contact; when written forms took weeks or months for delivery; when education was a luxury rather than an entitlement; when transportation was limited to foot or, perhaps, horseback; and when the staples of life taken for granted today— food, shelter, clothing, paper, etc.—assumed a value relatively unknown or possibly inconceivable to present-day Americans.

Only with this transformation to an earlier age can a family historian fully understand and appreciate some of the research problems he or she will encounter—to say nothing of solving those problems— when working with early baptismal information. The first step to this understanding and appreciation follows.

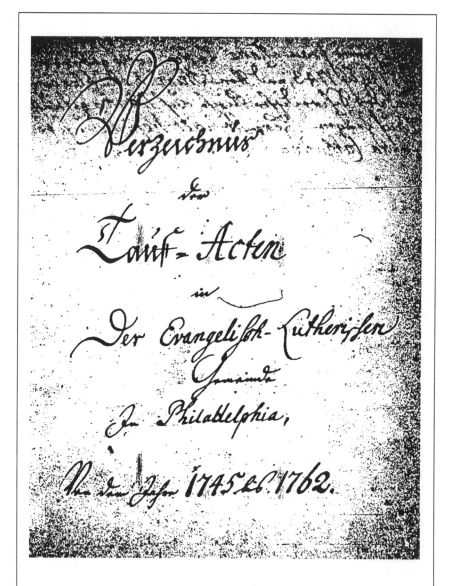

Title page from the first baptismal register of
St. Michael's and Zion Evangelical Lutheran Church,
Philadelphia, Pennsylvania.

Chapter 2

Baptismal Records

Baptismal records are important to the family historian because, ideally, they provide two or three essential pieces of information: the date that an ancestor's life began, the names of that ancestor's parents, and the name that person used throughout his life—for generations of the male descendants. Unfortunately, from the standpoint of genealogical research, eighteenth-century married women surrendered their maiden names in favor of their husbands' surnames.

The practice of keeping baptismal registers obviously did not begin in the wilds of Penn's Woods, but rather during the Reformation in Germany and Switzerland. On 24 May 1526, in Zurich, Ulrich Zwingli (1484–1531) urged the governing council to start maintaining church records because many people were not having their children baptized.[1] Registers from the same time period exist for Germany and, at a slightly later time, for England—the Church of England having been established in 1534. In September 1538, Henry VIII (1491–1547) issued an order stipulating that every parish priest was to maintain a record of all weddings, christenings, and burials. A threat of the return to Catholicism after Henry's death prompted Queen Elizabeth I (1533–1603) to reinforce the 1538 injunction in 1559.[2] The Catholic Church initiated its record-keeping in November 1563 as a result of the directives of the Council of Trent.[3]

All early records are subject to the vagaries of time, and Pennsylvania's baptismal records are no exception; gaps can be found in extant records, and many records are missing due in part to their having been lost or destroyed—a situation causing serious problems for historians pursuing their ancestry. Perhaps the least understood reason why many family historians cannot find those "missing" baptismal registers is that they were never kept.

Among the worthwhile groups of records to be found in Pennsylvania are the baptismal registers for the German and Swedish Lutheran churches, the German and Dutch Reformed churches and the Church of England (Anglican), known in 1784 and thereafter in the American Colonies as the Protestant Episcopal Church. Each of these denominations was the "established" or state church in its country of origin, and that state recognition afforded them an opportunity to develop a meaningful tradition of record-keeping without fear of persecution. When adherents to these faiths founded churches in Pennsylvania, they maintained the traditions of record-keeping they had earlier learned in Europe.

The family historian will encounter serious problems trying to locate baptismal records for denominations denied official recognition. Included among those churches are the Mennonites, Dunkards, Amish, English Baptists, and Presbyterians. These denominations had legitimate reasons to avoid maintaining records. First, church records were inadmissible in a court of law, making those records useless in terms of trying to help church members resolve legal problems. More important, many of the religious groups lacking official sanction were also heavily persecuted. The obvious question for these groups really became, "Why maintain lists of church members and pastoral acts only for the convenient use by antagonists for persecution?"

The post-Reformation history of the Catholic Church, both in Europe and in Pennsylvania, provides an interesting example to illustrate the problem. In those areas of Europe where the Catholic Church had gained official recognition, genealogists are able to track their lineage because the church maintained records. Descendants of English Catholics find it almost impossible to trace their ancestry because the Catholic Church was outlawed for a period of time in England.[4] During the reign of Elizabeth I (1558–1603), priests who held Mass did so at the risk of torture and death, and laymen who gave refuge to priests risked confiscation of their property. Under James I (1566–1625), thousands of Catholics were forced to surrender up to two-thirds of their estates because they persisted in clinging to their "papist" beliefs.[5]

Restrictive laws against Catholics were not limited to England. Laws enacted in 1715 and 1729 in Maryland stipulated that the children of Catholic marriages, when one partner died, were to be taken from the surviving parent for the purpose of a Protestant upbringing.[6] It cannot go unnoticed that Maryland was the colony founded by the avowed Roman Catholic Lord Baltimore for the resettlement of persecuted English Catholics.

The net effect of these and other similar laws was to force the Catholic Church in England and some of the American Colonies to operate underground. Services were held in private and, for fear of persecution, no records were kept.[7]

Several Catholic congregations were established in eighteenth-century Pennsylvania. The earliest, St. Joseph's Catholic, was erected in Philadelphia in 1733. A plaque at the church notes: "When in 1733 St. Joseph's Roman Catholic Church was founded . . . it was the only place in the entire English speaking world where public celebration of the Holy sacrifice of the Mass was permitted by law."[8]

Baptismal records for St. Joseph's Catholic begin in 1758, the same year the German Jesuit Ferdinand Farmer began his work in the parish.[9] Earlier baptismal records, from 1733 until 1758, do not exist, and it should not pass without note that during this time period—from 1733 until 1758—the parish priests were English. Father Farmer was called to St. Joseph's about the time the pastor of the church, Rev. Robert Harding, was beginning the process of establishing St. Mary's Catholic Church, the second Catholic Church in Philadelphia. No eighteenth-century baptismal records for St. Mary's are known to exist. Again, it must be noted that the early priests of this church were English.

In 1741 the Catholic congregation known as the "old mission church of St. Paul's at Goshenhoppen" was established in what is now Bally, Berks County, Pennsylvania. This congregation was almost exclusively German. The initial records for that church, begun in 1741,

were kept by the German Jesuit Father Theodore Schneider. The introduction to the published records for this church note: "Although
Goshenhoppen was not the first Catholic mission in Pennsylvania, its
registers are believed to be not only the oldest extant Catholic Church
registers in the state but the oldest in existence of the original thirteen
colonies."[10]

Given the disincentives to the maintenance of Catholic records in
England and Maryland, and given the existence of these early registers for two congregations in Pennsylvania, one cannot help but wonder if the tradition for keeping records for these Pennsylvania
Catholic churches may have some connection to the fact that priests
who were responsible for these two churches were German Jesuits
who came from an area of Europe where Catholics were not subjected
to restrictive laws and regulation.

The German Reformed, Dutch Reformed, and the Presbyterian are
three Pennsylvania denominations that share a similar doctrine. The
experience of these three churches was similar to that of the early
Catholics who settled in Pennsylvania in that both history and place
of origin determined what records were kept.

In 1588 the Dutch Reformed Church became the state church of
Holland; the Reformed Church in Germany achieved state recognition in 1648 as part of the settlement of the Thirty Years' War. Both of
these denominations kept good records in Europe, and they continued that practice in Pennsylvania. The Presbyterian Church was a recognized state church in Scotland only; in England the Presbyterians
were classified as dissenters or non-conformists.

Genealogists working on Presbyterian ancestors in Pennsylvania
will encounter significant difficulties in trying to locate early church
registers because only three pre-1760 Presbyterian church registers are
know to exist.[11] The absence of some Pennsylvania church registers
should not be too surprising given the history of the Presbyterian
Church in England and its relationship with the Anglican Church. A
serious dispute between the Presbyterian and Anglican churches over
the issue of church government persisted for more than two centuries.

The Church of England was an apostolic church—that is, its bishops claimed succession from the apostles, and leaders of this church
were adamant in their belief that the only true church was that church

which could claim succession from the disciples. The Presbyterian Church, organized around deacons, presbyters, and elders, claimed no apostolic succession and thus was not a true church in the eyes of the Church of England, its Sovereign, or Parliament.

The disagreement over church government reached its apogee during the reign of Charles I (1600–1649), who in the late 1630s attempted to impose an episcopal form of government on the Presbyterian Church in Scotland. His endeavor resulted in a war between Scotland and England that eventually lead to the English Civil War. Upon the defeat and subsequent execution of the king, the monarchy ended and England suffered under the rule of a military dictator. No single church dominated during the interregnum; the Presbyterians, Congregationalists (Puritans), and Quakers were on equal footing with the Church of England.

When the monarchy was restored in 1660, the Church of England was once again elevated to its former position as the official state church. In the following decade Parliament enacted a series of laws with the sole purpose of controlling—if not eradicating—non-conformist denominations perceived as being responsible, in part at least, for the English Civil War. Two of those laws were the Conventicle Acts of 1664 and 1670, which stated that any person above the age of sixteen who met with five or more people at any "assembly Conventicle or Meeting under colour or pretence of and exercise of Religion in other manner than according to the Liturgy and Practice of the Church of England,"[12] if found guilty, would be subjected to a series of penalties. For the first offense the fine was £5; for a second offense the fine was £10 or six months in jail; for a guilty party too poor to pay, the penalty was levied against those who met with him. Penalties for the third offense included transportation to "His Majesties Foreign Plantations,"—that would have been Virginia or New England— where the guilty party was held for seven years. Under this act, anyone transported to the colonies who escaped and returned to England without permission was convicted as a felon and sentenced to death. Penalties under these acts were also imposed upon the person who had preached at that meeting, and against the owner of the property where the meeting had been held. If found guilty, they were liable for a fine of £20 each. Justices of the Peace were authorized to enter any house or place where such a meeting took place, even to a point of breaking down the door to impose the laws of the realm.[13]

Another restrictive law passed by Parliament was the Uniformity Act of 1661, which had a significant impact on records kept by dissenters and non-conformists. The Uniformity Act restored the Church of England to its position as the official state church; the law also mandated that all ministers preaching in England agree to use the form of worship stipulated by the Church of England. The law specifically accepted "the *Book of Common Prayer* and the administration of the sacraments and other rites and ceremonies of this church together with the form and manner of ordaining and consecrating bishops, Priests and deacons heretofore in use and respectively established by an Act of Parliament" under Queen Elizabeth I. The net effect of this act was to outlaw Presbyterian and Congregationalist and Baptist ministers because they were not ordained by Bishops. According to section 10 of this same act, a £100 fine was imposed on any person who was not an ordained priest and who was found guilty of administering the sacraments.[14]

Penalties under the Act of Uniformity were a serious disincentive to maintaining baptismal registers; their existence would provide evidence that an unordained minister was in violation of the law—evidence that would be used in the courts to prosecute him. Thus, it should not be too surprising that Presbyterian and Baptist ministers in England did not develop a tradition of maintaining records of their pastoral acts.

The experience of the Moravian Church in England and in the Colonies stands in marked contrast to that of the Presbyterian Church. The Moravians were a small religious group who came to England from central Europe in the mid-1730s. The Moravian Church is an apostolic church whose bishops claim legitimate succession from the apostles. This similar background of apostolic belief enabled Parliament to enact a law on 12 May 1749 that, in essence, put the Moravian Church on an equal footing with the Church of England; on that date the Moravian Church became an established church both in England and British America.[15]

The Moravians had established an incredible tradition of record-keeping long before 1749, but the 1749 Act of Parliament enabled

Moravians to continue their tradition of maintaining records both in England and in America with the assurance that those records would not be used against them. At the same time it allowed Moravian records to be used as evidence in a court of law to support the claims of church members, and it legalized the pastoral acts of Moravian ministers.

In England, the Anglican Church and the Religious Society of Friends (Quakers) were the only denominations who kept consistently good records on a par with those of the Moravians. Unlike the Moravians, however, the Friends were a dissenting or non-conformist group. After the Church of England resumed its position as the official state church, the Quakers suffered along with the other dissenters. The disincentives to maintaining registers under the Act of Uniformity did not affect the Quakers because they did not baptize infants or give communion. Thus the Friends escaped penalties imposed for the administration of the sacraments, but they did not escape persecution. Parliament enacted a series of laws specifically directed against the Society of Friends, but those laws had no effect on the record-keeping traditions promoted by the Quakers during the interregnum.

Artistic representation of an early Christian adult baptism (Italian).
From *Enciclopedia Cattolica,* 2: 1023.

Chapter 3

The Base Position

Baptism is a rite of initiation for entrance into the Christian Church, and each denomination in eighteenth-century Pennsylvania gave that rite a different theological meaning. In recording baptismal information, the church makes a record of an activity that is perceived by many as being at the core of church's existence. The recordation of facts useful for genealogical research is only incidental to the sacrament of baptism.

Several elements surrounding baptism are essential to understanding its significance and practice as it relates to genealogical research. These elements include baptism's meaning, the proper candidates for baptism, confirmation, sponsors at baptism, emergency baptism, and conditional baptism. Several of these elements were the subject of a theological discussion that lead to the fracture or break-up of the western church. We know this crisis as the Reformation.

Depending on the denomination, some or all of the above-mentioned elements help to fix the information written into the baptismal record. For example, the meaning a denomination gives to baptism determines who is eligible for that rite within that group, and that interpretation may also determine the age at which the baptism is performed. Both of these considerations will influence the resultant

record. Likewise, the views of each denomination concerning sponsors determines who presents the child for baptism, and the record-
keeping traditions for that church may determine the usefulness of
that information. Thus it is imperative that the family historian exam-
ine the beliefs of each of the major religious groups in order to better
understand how those beliefs are reflected in baptismal records.

As practiced by the early Christian Church, baptism was considered a cleansing or washing away of original sin with water. The term
baptism comes from the Greek noun (βάπτισμα) meaning dipping or
washing.[1] Its basis in scripture can be found in the last chapter of Matthew, where Christ tells his disciples to "Go and make disciples of all
nations, baptizing them in the name of the Father and of the Son and
of the Holy Ghost. . ." (Matt. 28: 19–20). The last part of this verse,
among the most recognized in all of Christendom, is applied at baptism and is known as the Trinitarian Formula.

For three-quarters of the now almost two-thousand-year history of
the Christian Church, adherents of the Christian faith believed that
baptism constituted a complete remission from original sin. Baptism
was seen as the direct instrument of regeneration. Simply stated, it
was looked upon as being the only passageway to heaven; all who
died unbaptized were excluded.

The reward of baptism was not merely salvation. Baptism was also
seen as means of incorporating the recipient into the church, which is
the body of Christ. It was looked upon as a decisive act by which God
claims man almost miraculously, and "it cannot be repeated."[2] The
notion that baptism could not be repeated was one that had been ingrained into the traditions of early and medieval churches.

The precise rite of baptism is not defined in the New Testament;
rather, baptismal procedures were developed by the church. Baptism
as practiced by the early church was restricted to adults. In the third
century, someone who desired entrance into the church through baptism was presented to church leaders by "witnesses" who assured the
convert's worthiness for membership—that is, the sponsor attested to
the candidate's sincerity and suitablility. This initial presentation was
followed by an examination of the candidate. If the candidate was
found acceptable, then a course of instruction followed that could last
as long as three years. A final examination was conducted, after which
the candidate was baptized by immersion.[3]

The early church soon discovered that it had to deal with the problem of sin committed after baptism. In doing so, the church established a position whereby it had the right to grant remission from post-baptismal sin following confession and repentance.[4] This position eventually lead to the Sacrament of Penance, by which adherents to the faith were granted absolution from sin after confession and submission to penalties.

Forms and procedures gradually began to change. References in early church records show infant baptism beginning to emerge by the third century, but the practice was not universal. In the fourth century, early baptism was recommended for all infants as a protection from demons, heresy, and the danger of dying without the baptismal seal.[5] The rarity of adult baptism in the sixth century confirms the completion of the transition from adult to infant baptism.[6]

Baptism of infants necessitated an adaptation to the liturgy—specifically the interposition of one adult, ordinarily a parent, to speak and act on behalf of the newborn.[7] Ceremonies surrounding baptism also changed. White clothing was introduced to symbolize the innocence of new life, and candles were used to serve as a reminder of the purity of the soul. The newly-baptized child was anointed to symbolize his/her configuration to Christ. Other noted changes included the mode of baptism and its timing. Aspersion or sprinkling had replaced immersion.[8] Also, because infant baptism had come into its own, this sacrament generally took place shortly after the infant's birth.

In the early church it became customary to add the imposition of hands to the baptism, signifying the introduction of the Holy Spirit into the believer. This latter ceremony subsequently became know as confirmation, which was seen as a complement and completion of baptism, and was looked upon as a precursor to communion.[9] In the New Testament, its administration was reserved to the apostles and was later performed only by the bishop.[10] Upon the completion of these rites and ceremonies, the new Christian was admitted to communion for the first time. Baptism, confirmation, anointing, and communion in the early church were closely connected and occurred together around Easter.[11]

Over time the two rites of the western church, baptism and confirmation, were separated. Confirmation was fixed as one of the seven sacraments in the twelfth century. Confirmation in that epoch was administered to children when they reached age seven; it was felt that at age seven the child was old enough to understand and to learn the essentials of the Christian faith.[12] Like baptism, confirmation was never repeated; it was seen as leaving an indelible mark on the soul.

Like many of the elements surrounding baptism, sponsorship has roots in the early church. The pool of converts in the early church were pagan, and someone had to attest to their individual motives for joining the church and the sincerity of their beliefs. That person was the sponsor, whose true function in the early church was that of a witness.[13]

As the focus of the church changed from adult to infant baptism the role of the sponsor also changed. At infant baptism the sponsor spoke and acted for the child during the ceremony and accepted the infant from the hands of the priest after triple immersion.[14] In so doing the sponsor took on the obligation to foster the child's religious and moral development. The sole requirement of the sponsor was that he be a Christian, because only a Christian could make the baptismal confession for the child.[15] Generally the infant had only one sponsor who was of same sex, and frequently that sponsor was a parent.[16]

Several significant changes took place in the ninth century. The number of sponsors increased from one to three, two sponsors of the same sex as the child and a third of the opposite. In addition, the baptismal liturgy was altered to place greater emphasis on the role of the sponsors. The church also separated godparents from natural parents; it prohibited natural parents from acting as sponsors for their own children. The net result of these changes was to create two families, one natural and one spiritual, and these two families were prohibited from comingling through marriage. In 813, the Council of Mainz stipulated that "no one should take his own son or daughter from the font of baptism nor should he take as wife his goddaughter or co-mother, nor should he take as wife a woman whose son or daughter he led to confirmation."[17]

In the early Middle Ages, the church created a new role of spiritual kinship, and evidence surviving from this period often shows "spiritual kin" as socially prominent. It was not uncommon for kings and great princes to sponsor one another's children. People of lower social and economic status chose socially prominent people in the community as sponsors, as much for the potential help they could afford the parents as for the spiritual care they could give the child.[18] Evidence in certain areas of Europe shows spiritual kinship persisting up to the Reformation and even later.

The belief of the early church—baptism equals salvation—meant that seriously ill infants and adults who died without baptism were lost souls. It soon became apparent that some mechanism had to be established to save the dying, so the church developed the policy allowing that in the absence of a priest and in the case of necessity a layman or laywoman, pagan or even heretic, could baptize—provided he or she used the Trinitarian Formula and performed the baptism with good intent. That position was called emergency baptism, and evidence suggests that the church had established this practice by the third century. Around the year 300, St. Jerome (ca. 340–ca. 400) in the 38th canon decided ". . . that no rebaptism was necessary for those who had been baptized in an emergency by a layman but only that the persons so baptized should be brought to the Bishop for confirmation if they should survive."[19]

Provision for emergency baptism was absorbed into the literature of the church. John Myrc, in his manuals outlining instructions for parish priests, ordered that if the mother died in childbirth the midwife was to cut her open, extract the baby from the womb, and baptize it. She was to keep clean water available for this eventuality and was to repeat the phrase "I baptize you in the name of the Father, the Son and the Holy Ghost."[20] Other manuals told priests to frequently instruct their members in this form of baptism in the eventuality that they might be called upon to perform the rite in an emergency situation.

The church was adamant in its position that baptism was decisive and should not to be repeated. Emergency baptism gave laypersons the opportunity to perform the rite, an action creating a complicated predicament—that is, priests were possibly rebaptizing infants previously baptized by non-clergymen. Conditional baptism was the solution devised by the church to counteract the problem. This method of baptism placed a qualifier in the form of usage. In a conditional baptism the priest said, "If thou art not already baptized, I baptize thee in the name of the Father, and of the Son and of the Holy Ghost."[21] Conditional baptism was used in situations where doubts materialized as to the form or to the essentials of a previous baptism.

Evidence from canon law and other sources survives from the late medieval period to reconstruct a typical baptism on the eve of the Reformation. For the family historian it affords an opportunity for insight into baptismal practice for a typical late-fifteenth-century ancestor. It also provides an opportunity to see the changes that baptism underwent over the course of the first fifteen hundred years of the church and it affords an occasion to understand the interplay of the elements surrounding baptism. Finally, it establishes a point of reference for the many changes that would follow in the tumultuous sixteenth century.

Shortly after a child's birth the father assembled the sponsors— two females and a male for a girl, or two males and a female for a boy. Generally only a few people attended the baptism, the father, the godparents, and possibly older children in the family. As the baptism took place either on the day of birth or the following day, it is doubtful that the mother could attend because she was still recovering from the birth and was probably resting in the birth bed. The godmother or midwife carried the infant to the church door, where the priest met the baptismal party. The initial part of the ceremony took place outside, in front of the entrance to the church. The priest asked a few preliminary questions about the sex of the child and whether the child had been baptized. He then made the sign of the cross on the infant's forehead and placed his hands on the head of the child, saying a prayer. Salt, over which an exorcism had been said, was placed in the mouth of the child to symbolize the reception of wisdom.[22] The priest then performed an exorcism to drive out any demons lurking in the newborn; this act was followed by another signing of the cross, and the ears and nostrils of the child were touched with saliva.[23]

The next part of the ceremony took place inside the church at the baptismal font. The priest took the infant by the hand and led him/her into the church to the font located near the door. This action symbolized the fact that baptism was considered entrance into the church. At the font the priest placed his right hand upon the child and asked the infant's name. He then blessed the infant with chrism (anointed oil) in the form of the cross and sprinkled the newborn three

A panel depicting infant baptism,
from the doors of the baptistry of St. John the Baptist, Florence, Italy.
The bronze doors are the artistry of Andrea Pisano (ca. 1290–1348).
From *Enciclopedia Cattolica*, 2: 1024.

times using the Trinitarian Formula. The child was then taken from the font and given to the principal sponsor whose name the child received. The child was again signed with the cross and clothed with a white vestment symbolizing the innocence of new life, and a lighted candle was placed in the newborn's hand to symbolize the purity of the soul.[24]

From the font the party moved to the altar for the profession of faith, where the sponsors answered for the infant. The role of the sponsors was primarily spiritual. They would be responsible for teaching the infant the *Pater Noster* (Lord's Prayer), the *Ave Maria*, and the *Credo* (Creed). The priest tested the sponsors' knowledge of these prayers as part of the baptismal ceremony.[25] In the eyes of the church the sponsors were the child's guardians and they were charged with the responsibility ". . . to ensure that he faithfully executes the promises he has made through your words. It is your duty to remind him of his great obligations and urge him to live up to them just as soon as he is old enough to understand and lift his heart up to God."[26]

According to church law, sponsors could not be related by blood or marriage to parents; therefore, listed among those who were not eligible as sponsors were uncles, aunts, cousins, grandparents, or people who might enter the family through marriage in the future. The parents had to be careful in their selection of sponsors, and they frequently chose someone from the community, such as a fellow guildsman or perhaps a socially prominent person who would be helpful to both the infant and the family.[27]

As Barbara Hanawalt notes in her book, *Growing Up in Medieval London*: "From the infant's point of view baptism was probably not comfortable. The ceremonies outside the church and at the font and the trip home could leave the infant chilled. The salt was hardly pleasant and the water in the font could be terribly cold in the winter. One presumes that most babies cried through much of the ceremony."[28]

The Catholic Church

The position of the Catholic Church on baptism altered little as a result of the Reformation. The Council of Trent, the belated response of the Catholic Church to the Protestant Reformation, reaffirmed the age-old position of baptism as salvation from original sin. Traditionally the Catholic Church has always been adamant in its position that all who died unbaptized, including infants, are denied entrance into heaven. The commitment of the church to this doctrine is so fixed that even a fetus is unsaved, as is evidenced by the fact that a Catholic priest is permitted to baptize an unborn infant.[29]

Baptism in the Catholic Church is open to everyone, and parental membership in the church is not a prerequisite. Infants of non-Catholic parents can be baptized without the consent of the parents if the child is in danger of death. If there is no imminent danger of death, then the consent of only one parent is necessary for the baptism to occur.[30] The openness of baptism in the Catholic Church allowed eighteenth-century Pennsylvania Catholic priests to baptize the infants of Protestants. As is evidenced by the registers of Pennsylvania's early Catholic churches, priests noted that some parents were Protestant or non-Catholic.

The presence of sponsors at baptisms was ratified in 1563 by the Council of Trent, but the Council reduced the number of sponsors from three to one or, at most, two persons. The church also took the position that the presence of a sponsor was not essential to the administration of the rite.[31]

The Catholic Church stipulated the exact information that the parish priest should record in the church register: name of the person baptized, the officiating minister, parents and sponsors, and the place and day on which the baptism was peformed. No mention was made of a requirement to record the date of birth because the church was concerned with maintaining permanent records of baptismal ceremonies only; some registers for Pennsylvania's early Catholic churches, however, show that priests also gathered birth information and recorded it as well.[32]

Extant eighteenth-century records for Catholic congregations in Pennsylvania follow the stipulated form. Baptismal records of the St. Joseph's Catholic Church in Philadelphia and the Goshenhoppen Church in Berks County, for example, follow the established pattern, providing names of the infant, father and mother, dates of birth and baptism, names of sponsors and, generally, the location where the baptism occurred.

The Catholic Church in early Pennsylvania retained the position adopted by the early church with regard to emergency baptism. Lay or emergency baptisms do not appear with great frequency in Pennsylvania's early Catholic Church registers, which should not be too surprising, since most emergency baptisms were probably performed by laymen, parents, or a midwife—none of whom had access to the church register where the baptism could be recorded. In those cases where an emergency necessitated a lay baptism, and where the record actually found its way into the church register, the entry usually identifies the reason for the act. A typical example is the entry found in the

Goshenhoppen register for Peter Ruffner, son of Christian and Mary Odilia Rufner. This record notes that Peter was born 24 January 1767 and "was baptized privately by its father on account of danger of death, ceremonies supplied in the church on 22 February, sponsors Peter Kass and his wife."[33]

The terminology "ceremonies supplied," as noted above, is an expression frequently found in Catholic registers. In Ruffner's case, the infant was baptized privately because, as the record states, death was imminent. Actually the child survived but was not rebaptized; instead, the priest recognized the prior baptism and "ceremonies" were "supplied." On 22 February 1767 the sponsors, who were probably not present when Christian Ruffner baptized his son, made vows before the priest on behalf of the child.

The baptismal record for Philip James Bisschof, son of Peter and Charlotte Bisschof, provides a slightly different but equally useful example. Philip, born 1 May 1768, was "baptized privately by its father in danger of death, baptized conditionally August 28." Sponsors were Henry Fretter and Mary Bisschof.[34] The date Peter Bisschof baptized his son is not provided; 28 August 1768 is the date when the priest performed the conditional baptismal ceremony—that is to say, on 28 August the priest rebaptized the child with the qualifying statement "If thou art not already baptized. . . ." In this instance, the priest had some reason to question the form Peter Bischof had used in the emergency baptism of his son and he, the priest, felt it was necessary to conditionally rebaptize the child.

Variations of the conditional baptism can also be found in Catholic registers. An entry for the baptism of Margaret Murray, born 12 April 1763, daughter of Hugh and Elizabeth Murray, is a case in point. The child was baptized conditionally on 25 March 1767, almost four years after her birth. Sponsors for the ceremony were James Welsh and Anna Roage. The record notes that the father was a Protestant and that the child "had been baptized by a Presbyterian minister."[35] Again, for some unknown reason, the priest questioned validity of the original baptism and conditionally rebaptized the child.

Illegitimate births in early Catholic registers are not readily identified because priests did not use the terminology normally associated with questionable births. In fact, the Catholic Church mandated the format for recording illegitimate births. Priests were to record the name of the mother if the fact of her motherhood was publicly known with certainty, or if she voluntarily requested—in writing and in the presence of witnesses—that the church records document her relationship to the child. The same procedures governed identity of the father; otherwise, the baptized child was to be recorded as the child of an unknown father or of unknown parents.[36]

Given this mandate, entries in Pennsylvania's early Catholic registers that fail to identify the father probably imply questionable births. The baptismal record for John Adam Jung is typical of this kind of entry. John Adam Jung, of—the space where the father's name normally apears is left blank—and Anna Jung, born eight months ago, baptized 13 May 1781, in the chapel; sponsors, John Adam Schmitt and his wife Margaret.[37]

The format as prescribed by the church for recording illegitimate births also helps to explain a record found in the registers of St. Joseph's Catholic Church in Philadelphia. Archibald Asky was baptized on 3 April 1777, four years after his birth. The sponsors listed are Leonard and Mary Anna Lasher. Both of Archibald's parents are identified as "unknown."[38] A genealogist working with this record might conclude that the child might have been an abandoned "foundling," or that maybe the priest merely failed to remember or to record the names of the parents. The last option is unlikely given the other pertinent details the priest recorded about the child and sponsors. The more plausible explanation can be found among the guidelines for recording illegitimate births: ". . . in the case of an illegitimate birth, the mother and the father were to be recorded only if their identity was known with certainty. Otherwise they were recorded as unknown."[39] Given this church-mandated format for recording questionable births, Archibald Asky was probably born of parents whose union had not been officially sanctioned through the Sacrament of Marriage.

Confirmation is seen as the completion of baptism. When a child of Catholic parents comes of age, he or she assumes responsibility for his or her own spiritual welfare. Confirmation, one of the twelve sacraments of the Catholic Church, was fixed as a doctrine in the sixteenth century by the Council of Trent.[40] The principle stipulated that children from the age of seven to twelve were eligible to receive the Sacrament of Confirmation. As practiced by the Catholic Church, the bishop administers that rite by the imposition of hands and the anointing of the forehead with consecrated oil.[41]

Because confirmation rites had to be administered by a bishop, it is doubtful that any Catholics were confirmed in Pennsylvania prior to 15 August 1790, the date John Carroll of Maryland (1735–1815) was consecrated as the first American Bishop of the Roman Catholic Church. Prior to the creation of the American Diocese in 1789, American Catholics were under the jurisdiction the English Catholic Church, and pre-1790 confirmation records for Americans, if any exist, would be found in England.

Chapter 4

First Removed

The Lutherans and Moravians, the two oldest Protestant denominations, together with the Anglicans (members of the Church of England, and more recently known in the in the United States as the Protestant Episcopal Church) are identified in this chapter as "first removed." These three were among the first religious coalitions to break ties with the Catholic Church, but that is not the reason why they are grouped together here. Rather, these sects are clustered under a single heading based on the similarity of their philosophy of baptism and because the changes they made in the doctrine of baptism were less radical than the changes made by denominations who followed in the Reformed or Anabaptist and Baptist traditions. The Methodists are also included as an addendum to the "first removed"— by virtue of their formation in 1784 as direct descendants of the Church of England.

The Lutheran Church

Martin Luther (1483–1546) retained the doctrine of baptism as salvation. In his Catechism, Luther noted: "No one is baptized in order to become a prince, but as the word says 'to be saved.' To be saved, we know, is nothing else than to be delivered from sin, death and the

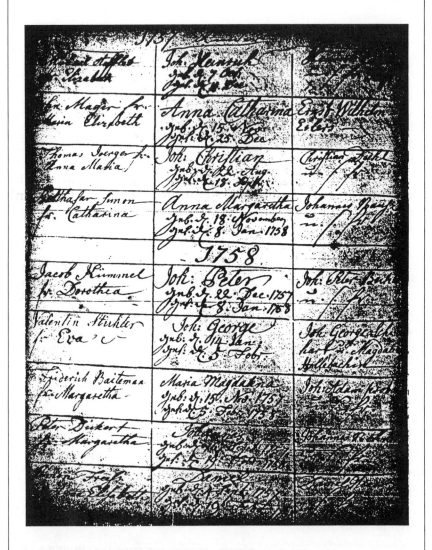

New Hanover Lutheran Church, Montgomery County, Pennsylvania,
is the oldest German Lutheran Church in North America (founded ca. 1717).
Baptismal records were initiated by Rev. Henry Melchior Muhlenberg in 1742.
This page of the New Hanover baptismal register dates from 1757–58.

devil and to enter into the kingdom of Christ and live with him forever."[1] In Luther's view salvation through baptism comes from God and is not a work of man or, for that matter, the church. He attacked the Catholic concept of baptism on the grounds it was mechanical—that it was not the washing of water that saved man, but God, through his word.[2]

Luther believed that what man brings to baptism is his faith; baptism without faith is of no use. The promise God granted in baptism is received only by faith that comes to us through God's word and His Spirit. Luther vehemently denied penance as man's salvation for post-baptismal sin. He argued that faith helps man to survive the daily tests of sin and suffering. According to Luther, a Christian's baptism is not expendable—it is not used up—baptism saves man when he strays.[3]

Luther also changed the ceremony by simplifying it. In his opinion, putting salt in the mouth and spittle and clay into the ears and nose, along with anointing the breast and shoulders with oil, signing the crown of the head with chrism, wearing a christening robe, and placing a burning candle in the hand, were all embellishments added by man. In Luther's view, these things were external and were not necessary to baptism; they were not "the sort of devices and practices from which the devil shrinks and flees. . . ."[4]

The role of sponsors at baptism was left intact. Because of the seriousness of the ceremony, Luther felt it was the parents' responsibility to chose sponsors who were decent, moral, earnest, and sober. What Luther did reject and alter was the Catholic idea of spiritual kinship. It was his notion that Catholics had concocted new degrees of relationship that did not really exist, because ". . . in baptism we are all brothers in Christ."[5] It was on this basis that Luther invalidated the prohibitions established by the Catholic Church against marriage between spiritual and natural kin.

For Lutherans, the prohibition restricting family members from sponsoring infants was lifted. This change may not have been significant in terms of doctrine and theology, but it is noteworthy for the family historian because this change made it possible for relatives to claim spiritual responsibility for their kin, and it allowed their names to appear in the Lutheran church registers of Germany and Pennsylvania.

Martin Luther retained the practice of emergency baptism, but he eliminated conditional baptism from Lutheran Church practice. According to Luther, " . . . conditional baptism turned the sacrament of baptism into a matter of uncertainty while baptism is and should be the most certain assurance of man's salvation."[6]

The traditional Catholic doctrine that accepted baptism as entrance into the church was not altered by Luther, and he held to the belief that the right to partake of the Lord's Supper came from baptism, not confirmation. At the same time, Luther rejected the Catholic view of confirmation and its doctrine of confirmation as a sacrament. Luther believed that the church should bear responsibility for instructing its members, especially the children, in the tenets of the faith and to prepare them for admittance to communion. For Luther, the instruction that preceded the rite was the most important part of confirmation.[7]

The journals of Rev. Henry Melchior Muhlenberg (1711–1787) contain comments about the connection between baptism and confirmation. The Lutheran practice of confirmation as described by Muhlenberg indicates that Lutheran ministers in Pennsylvania confirmed new members with the laying on of hands. An April 1764 entry in Muhlenberg's journals noted that on Good Friday he confirmed sixty-two young people. "[T]hey renewed their baptismal covenant and made their profession of faith and I confirmed them with prayer and the laying on of hands."[8]

The Swedes were the earliest practitioners of Lutheranism in Pennsylvania, having settled on the banks of the Delaware River in 1638. Prior to Rev. Muhlenberg's 1742 arrival in Philadelphia, Swedish Lutheran ministers had already established five Lutheran churches, two of which were in Pennsylvania—Gloria Dei in Philadelphia and St. Gabriel's at the present town of Douglassville, Amity Township in Berks County. The evangelical endeavors of Swedish Lutheran pastors extended beyond its own parishioners. John Dylander, a Swedish Lutheran minister, assisted in helping to establish the German Lutheran congregations in both Philadelphia and in Germantown.

Unfortunately, baptismal records for these early Swedish congregations are no longer extant. The earliest records to be found for the

Swedish Lutheran Church in Philadelphia begin in 1750. Baptismal entries in the register of Gloria Dei are similar to other Lutheran church registers with two exceptions: many of the entries in the Swedish registers provide a location for the family and almost all have three or more sponsors. A typical entry includes the following information: William Rambo of Wicaco, born the 23rd of February, baptized the 9th of March 1754: his father is John Rambo, the mother Elizabeth Rambo; witnesses Jane Nedermark, Mary Swanson and the father.[9]

Baptism as practiced by the Swedish and German Lutheran churches in Pennsylvania was very open. In fact, early Pennsylvania Lutheran records contain no evidence to suggest that obstructions were raised to limit its availability. Church membership was not a requirement, as verified by the baptismal record for Maria Catharina Huber. On 30 April 1763, Maria Catharina's father, Johannes Huber, asked Rev. Muhlenberg to baptize his infant daughter and, at the same time, to register his name for instruction and confirmation.[10] Further evidence in Pennsylvania records also shows that "preparation" was not a prerequisite for sponsors. An entry in the registers for St. Michael's and Zion Lutheran Church in Philadelphia notes the baptism on 9 November 1756 of Maria Bader, age four, daughter of Johannes and Catharine Bader. Rev. Brunnholtz added this comment: "[N]either of them [the parents] have as yet partaken of the Sacrament [baptism] but have promised to do so with a solemn handshake. The sponsors have also promised to prepare themselves."[11] In 1780, the Ministerium refused to impose a restriction against baptizing illegitimate children whose parents had not made a confession of their sins.[12]

Inconsistencies and irregularities in the information recorded by Lutheran ministers in eighteenth-century church registers confirms that the Lutheran Church obviously had not prescribed a format for recording baptismal information comparable to the rules earlier established by the Catholic Church. Generally speaking, Lutheran ministers recorded the name of the infant, the names both parents, dates of birth and baptism, and the names of sponsors. Rev. Henry Muhlenberg's entry for the baptism of Margaretha Simon in Philadelphia follows the standard format: Johannes Simon and Catharina; Margaretha, born the 8th October 1763, baptized the 4th December 1763; sponsors Ludewig Wengler and Margaretha, his wife.[13]

Exceptions to this format are numerous. Although it is possible that some records have been lost or destroyed, many of the early ministers recorded no information, as is evidenced by the absence of church registers. These early ministers, however, were working under most difficult circumstances at best. When records were kept, some ministers recorded the name of the infant, date of baptism, and the name of the father only, ignoring the name of the mother, date of birth, and the names of sponsors.

Other early Lutheran ministers added unusual information of potential interest to family historians. For example, Rev. Peter Brunnholtz baptized Friedrich Ludwig Krusins, son of Jurg Ludwig

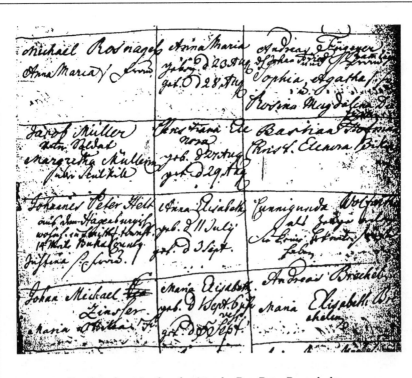

Baptismal entries, handwritten by Rev. Peter Brunnholtz,
St. Michael's and Zion Lutheran Church, Philadelphia.

and Margaretha Krusins, on 27 December 1756. Brunnholtz added to the entry in the register of St. Michael's and Zion Lutheran Church in Philadelphia, "new comers from Edelmanischen Seckendorf." In addition, Rev. Brunnholtz' church register provides the place of origin for twenty-one German immigrants, but his comments are not restricted to places of origin in Germany. The record for the baptism of Johan Martin Förster's daughter Maria Magdalena notes that the parents had been in the country seven years and lived at "Point no Point." Appended to the 5 October 1756 entry for the baptism of Barbara George is the statement that the child's parents, Peter and Susannah George, for six years were located at "Harris's ferry on the Susquehanna." Rev. Brunnholtz was so thorough in his record-keeping that his premature death in 1757 is probably still mourned by genealogists working on German families.[14]

The Protestant Episcopal Church

Rev. Henry Muhlenberg, in his journals, described the Anglicans as his "nearest and best friends." Indeed, a reader going through his writings soon discovers that in Pennsylvania a close cooperation existed between the Lutherans, both Swedish and German, and the Anglican Church, frequently identified by Muhlenberg as the "English High Church."[15] This cooperation should not come as a great surprise. These two denominations shared a similarity of belief and doctrine on many spiritual issues.

Their ideas were similar concerning baptism. Like the Lutherans, the Anglicans believed baptism provided salvation from sin. Baptism was the mysterious instrument of regeneration authored by God. As the *Book of Common Prayer* notes, "The necessity of Holy Baptism to salvation is so urgent and the blessing conferred by it so great, infants should be brought to the font as early as possible."[16]

The Anglicans also held the traditional belief that baptism constituted entrance into the church, and public baptism for infants was encouraged because the congregation's presence would testify to the reception of the newly-baptized into Christ's Church. The church did provide for the baptism of infants at home, identified as "private baptism," and after 1661 also provided for adult baptism—available to those people who could answer for themselves.[17]

The administration of the Sacrament of Baptism was strictly defined by the *Book of Common Prayer*. In the case of public baptism, parents were to notify the curate or pastor before the child was brought to the church. Generally the baptism was performed immediately after the last lesson at morning or evening prayer. At the font the pastor asked if the child had been previously baptized. If a negative response was given, then the minister baptized the child by asperison using the Trinitarian Formula.[18]

Sponsors were present at the baptism and made the vows on behalf of the child. Initially the Anglican Church continued the Catholic practice of three sponsors—two godfathers and one godmother for every male child, and one godfather and two godmothers for every female child. After 1661, however, the number of sponsors was reduced to two. The Church of England also adopted (or at least continued) the Catholic prohibition of parents acting as godparents for their own children. This position was retained until 1865.[19]

Anglicans continued the ancient practice of emergency baptism, and this retention of lay baptism allowed for private baptism at home. Directives in the *Book of Common Prayer* state that if the child is in danger of dying, prayers are to be omitted and the child is to be baptized at once. Furthermore, if a minister of the Church of England is approached and is asked to baptize a dying infant, and he either refuses or delays the baptism and the child dies, then he, the minister, could be suspended from his duties.[20]

The Anglicans, unlike the Lutherans, retained the Catholic tradition of conditional baptism; however, the pastor was to be judicious in its use. He was not supposed to administer conditional baptism hastily "as a means of escaping from a difficulty."[21]

The Catholic belief that baptism should be open to everyone was retained by the Church of England. The directives of the church stipulated that a minister could not refuse baptism to anyone who sought the rite. The consequence for refusal was suspension by the bishop.[22] Thus, in eighteenth-century Pennsylvania, anyone wanting to have a child baptized—even the follower of another faith—could approach an Anglican minister knowing that the request would be granted.

The Anglicans also retained the rite of confirmation, which was considered a prerequisite for communion. At the baptism of infants, the minister directed the sponsors of the child to assure that the child would be brought to confirmation. No specific age when the rite was to be performed was set by the church, but it was understood that the child must have some intelligent understanding of the duties he/she was about to undertake.[23]

The Church of England kept the centuries-old tradition that the bishop should perform the rite of confirmation.[24] This position had significant implications for the Anglican Church in the American Colonies prior to 1787. Simply stated, before 1787 there were no Anglican bishops in the Colonies who could confirm church members. Any member of the Church of England who desired confirmation had to journey to England for its administration. Thus, no pre-1787 confirmation records exist for members of the Church of England in American record repositories.

Under the rules of the Church of England, only confirmed members of the church could receive communion; consequently, at least technically, communion could be given to only those Anglicans who had come to America as members already confirmed in the church or to those who had returned to England for confirmation. The fact that Anglican clergy were prevented from offering communion to members of their Pennsylvania churches helps to explain one of Rev. Muhlenberg's journal entries. On 1 April 1753, Muhlenberg wrote that he had buried Thomas How, one of his neighbors, on that day. Mr. How was born in 1681 in Hertfordshire, England, had come to Pennsylvania early in the eighteenth century, and was a member of St. James Episcopal Church in New Providence, Montgomery County. Muhlenberg noted that ". . . How never received Holy Communion yet he always considered himself a member of the English Church."[25] The reason Thomas How "never received communion" had nothing to do with the sincerity of his beliefs; rather, he had probably not been confirmed in the church prior to his departure from England.

Baptismal information recorded by the parish priest in Anglican church registers was prescribed by law. Passed by Parliament in 1603, the law stated that each parish priest and chapel was to have a parchment book wherein the day and year of every christening was to be written. Each sabbath ". . . immediately after morning and evening

A page from the first baptismal record book of
Christ Church, Philadelphia, started in 1709.
These 1715 notations were probably entered by Evan Evans, Rector.

prayers the minister and church warden shall take the said book out of the coffer and the minister in the presence of the church warden shall record in said book the names of all persons christened together with the names and surnames of the parents."[26] Typical entries for eighteenth-century Anglican baptisms in Pennsylvania follow the format stipulated in the 1603 law; in Church of England registers the information to be found is limited to the name of the infant, names of parents, and dates of birth and baptism. Little if any deviation from this format can be found in Pennsylvania's Anglican church records. Although sponsors were present at Church of England baptisms, Anglican ministers did not record their names—probably because the listing of sponsors' names was not mandated in the 1603 law (or earlier), and thus that information was not traditionally kept.

Genealogists looking for pre-1776 Anglican church records in Pennsylvania will encounter serious difficulties. On the eve of the American Revolution, twenty Anglican churches had been established in seven Pennsylvania counties. Pre-Revolutionary War baptismal records can be found for only six of the twenty congregations. It is probable, certainly possible, that the early records for the remaining fourteen congregations were casualties of the American Revolution.

At their ordination, Anglican ministers promised before God their obedience to the King of England, who was the head of their church and "the Defender of their Faith." The decision on the part of the American Colonies to declare their independence from King George III (1738–1820) put Anglican clergy into personal turmoil. On one hand, many ministers wanted to continue servicing their parishes, but on the other hand, if they did so they violated their oath.[27] Their dilemma was complicated by the fact that in Pennsylvania their salary was not derived from local tax revenues as was the case in Maryland, New York, and Virginia, where the Church of England had been designated the state church. Anglican clergy in Pennsylvania were paid by the Society for the Propagation of the Gospel in Foreign Parts, which was based in London.[28] Nine of the ten ministers then serving Anglican congregations left their Pennsylvania churches for England, Canada, or Bermuda. The lone exception was Rev. William White, assistant pastor of Christ Church in Philadelphia. In 1777 he became the chaplain of the Continental Congress, and ten years later, in 1787, he

was consecrated as the first American Bishop of the Protestant Episcopal Church.[29]

The turmoil experienced within the Anglican Church during the
American War for Independence was not limited to the clergy. Many
church members also remained loyal to King George and either returned to England or fled to Canada, and it is possible that many of
the early baptismal records for Anglican churches in Pennsylvania
disappeared with them, perhaps taken by the pastors or church members on their flight from the American Colonies.

For the duration of the Revolutionary War, many Anglican
churches lay dormant. Simply stated, they were abandoned until the
church reorganized in 1784 as the Protestant Episcopal Church. Not
surprisingly, many of the extant baptismal registers for Pennsylvania's Episcopalian churches begin in that year.

The Moravian Church

The Moravian Church has its roots in central Europe. The church
was founded in 1457 in Kunewalde, Moravia, by followers of the
martyred John Huss (1369?–1415), making it the oldest know Protestant denomination. At the beginning of the sixteenth century, when
Martin Luther began the Reformation in Germany, historians estimate
the Moravian church membership to be about 200,000. The early
Moravian Church had been reduced to fifteen parishes by the end
of the seventeenth century as a result of the wars of the Counter-
Reformation.[30]

Those Moravians who settled in Pennsylvania in the early- to mid-
eighteenth century were members of the renewed Moravian Church.
The theology of the renewed church combined many doctrines of the
early church with the ideas of Count Zinzendorf (1700–1760), whose
thinking was heavily influenced by Lutheran Pietism. In terms of baptism, the Moravians held to the view that baptism was salvation.[31] Infant baptism was seen by early church leaders as the initial entry into
the church, but it was not automatic. Children had to be brought up in
the faith to become members of the spiritual body of Christ.[32]

One of Zinzendorf's contributions to Moravian doctrine was the
rejection of the Catholic concept that children who die unbaptized are
unsaved. He held to the belief that "all children, even those unbap-

tized, are the objects of the grace of God in Christ. Should one die before baptism, he therefore is not damned but through the blood of Christ he is saved."[33]

The custom of the Moravian Church in the mid-eighteenth century was to baptize, by aspersion, the infants of church members shortly after birth. At Moravian settlements in Pennsylvania and in Germany, the Moravian Brethren and Sisters were awakened to attend the baptism of children born at night.[34] Understandably, this policy of baptizing infants almost immediately after birth was abandoned. Evidence found in Moravian church registers suggests that baptisms occurring later in the eighteenth century took place within a day or two of birth.

At a typical eighteenth-century Moravian baptism, five witnesses or sponsors were present who, with the minister, laid their hands on the infant and ". . . fervently commended in prayer . . . the gracious preservation of God from all evil and from the power of sin and satan."[35]

The Moravian Church was actively evangelistic toward natives of the American Colonies during the eighteenth century, and the work of the church and its several Indian missionaries met with some success as a number of former heathens became members of the Moravian Church. Baptisms for children native Americans who had become members of the Moravian Church differed from baptisms for infants of other church members. A form of exorcism was used for American Indian baptisms: ". . . all powers of darkness were commanded in the name of Jesus to depart from the baptized."[36]

Private baptism as practiced by Catholics and Lutherans was discouraged in the Moravian Church. Since baptism was considered the addition of a new member to the church, Moravian ministers were encouraged to incorporate the baptism as part of the service of public worship whenever possible.[37] The active participation of the congregation was seen as a commitment on their part to help the parents raise the child in the church and in "the nurture and the admonition of the Lord."[38]

The Moravian Church held to the traditional belief that confirmation was a prerequisite for participation in the Sacrament of the Lord's Supper. This position was consistent with the view of the church that

The 1751 Moravian baptism of Indians
in the chapel at Bethlehem, Pennsylvania.

From *Bethlehem on the Lehigh*, 13.

baptism was not automatic; children had to be brought up in the faith. Candidates for confirmation were instructed in the doctrines of the church and Christianity. Following a public examination, the candidate made a profession of faith before the congregation.[39]

The Moravians incorporated the use of the "lot" in the confirmation process as well as in other aspects of their daily lives. The lot did not have its origins in the old Moravian Church; its use was introduced by Count Zinzendorf early in the eighteenth century. The lot was a process for determining the will of God, and the process was fairly simple. As it related to confirmation, a statement favoring the confirmation was placed upon one slip of paper, a statement against was placed upon a second slip of paper, and a third slip was left blank. The three pieces of paper were inserted into three tubes. After the tubes were mixed, an answer was drawn from one of the tubes. An affirmative response allowed the candidate to be confirmed; if a negative response was drawn, the candidate was refused confirmation; a blank response was indefinite, meaning that the potential confirmand could resubmit a request for confirmation, to be decided by the lot at a later date.[40] Moravians frequently held a communion conference preceding a communion service where, among other things, the question of confirmation was submitted to the lot. If a favorable decision was drawn from one of the tubes, the candidate was confirmed before the group with the laying on of hands.[41]

Like their Lutheran and Anglican/Episcopalian counterparts, the Moravians had a fairly open concept of baptism, and their records show that they baptized the infants of non-Moravians. However, unlike the Catholics, Lutherans, and Anglicans, they would not baptize the infants of everyone who approached and requested administration of the sacrament. Their hesitation was the product of their religious beliefs and their attitudes about nurturing children in the church. The Moravians thought that conferring baptism on the child placed partial responsibility for the spiritual welfare of the infant directly upon the church as well as the parents. Therefore, if the minister was not personally acquainted with the child's parents or other family members, or if he could not be assured that the child would be brought up in the knowledge of the Christian faith, he would politely refuse to perform the rite.

The format used by the Moravians for recording baptismal information differs in some ways from the order used by Lutherans and Episcopalians. Each baptismal entry in a Moravian register is numbered. That is, each entry is given a sequential number starting at the beginning of the register with the number one. The name of the infant, the names of both parents, dates of baptism and birth, as well as the names of each of the sponsors, are written in the register; sometimes the entry also discloses the place where the baptism took place. In addition, Moravian records always provide the name of the minister who performed the ceremony—information not often found in baptismal records for other church denominations.

The record for Magdalena Graff (reproduced below) as found in the register of the Emmaus Moravian Church in Lehigh County is fairly typical, but it also includes an additional detail unique to mid-eighteenth-century Moravian baptismal records.

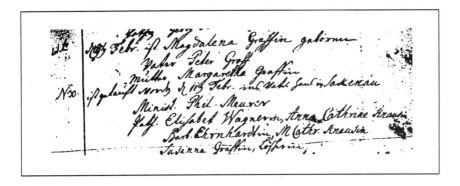

This record translates as: "[entry] #30, born 8 February 1748, Magdalena Graffin, father Peter Graff, mother Margaretha Graffin, baptized 11 February in the father's house in Saucon. The minister: Brother Philip Meurer, sponsors: Elisabeth Wagner, Anna Catharina Knauss, Barbara Ehrenhardt, M. Cath. Knaussin and Susanna Graffin."[42] Five sponsors were present at the baptism and all were of the same gender as the infant.

This practice of limiting sponsors to the same sex as the child was later modified, as is evidenced by other entries found in the same register. The entry numbered 332 recorded the baptism of Ludwig

Giering, born 12 January 1800, baptized Sunday, 12 January 1800, son of Brother Andreas Giering, Jr., and his wife Maria, born Gunther. The sponsors were: Brother Andreas Giering, Sr., the grandfather; Sister Maria Christ. Bohler, born Krohn; Sister Catharine Giering, born Romig; and Brother Ludwig Friedrich Bohler. The minister who performed the rite was Brother Ludwig Friedrich Bohler.[43] Genealogists should note that Moravian baptismal records often include married women's maiden names, both for a child's mother and for female sponsors.

"Brother" and "Sister" are terms frequently found in Moravian baptismal records. They do not designate relationships within the natural family of the child; rather they identify those present at the baptism as members of the Moravian Church. The official title of the Moravian Church is the Unitas Fratrum, or United Brethren. The Moravian Church is a Brethren Church. As such, its members are repeatedly identified in early church records as either Brother or Sister.

The Methodist Church

The Methodist Church is an offshoot of the Church of England. In the 1730s, three Anglican ministers, John Wesley (1703–1791), Charles Wesley (1707–1788), and George Whitefield (1714–1770), took a different approach to faith. Each of these men had experienced a personal conversion and had redefined their faith on that basis. In essence, they believed that man was a depraved creature who would perish without Christ as his Savior; to gain salvation he must make a personal decision for commitment to accept Christ.[44] Their coupling of this new theology with an aggressive ministry throughout England and the American Colonies soon produced a following that was organized into societies. The name they adopted for their movement, Methodist, was one that they had used during their college days at Oxford—taken from the Bible, wherein John defined a methodist as "one who lives according to the method laid down in the Bible."[45]

John Wesley was quite reluctant to have his followers break away from the Church of England, but the schism became inevitable after the American Colonies severed ties with Great Britain. On 1 September 1784, after serious thought and deliberation, Wesley ordained three men as deacons and elders who then traveled to America. At

a conference in Baltimore on 25 December 1784, these men in turn ordained Francis Asbury (1745–1816) along with twelve additional
men.[46] As a result of this conference, the Methodist Church was officially set apart from the Church of England and became a denomination in its own right.

Baptism, according to John Wesley, was a sign of the regeneration
that had already occurred in the Christian, and it was to be administered to infants to strengthen their faith. The Methodist discipline de-
fines baptism as ". . . not only a sign of profession and a mark of
difference whereby Christians are distinguished from others who are
not baptized; but it is also a sign of regenerated birth."[47] Parents were
urged to dedicate their children to the Lord in baptism as early as possible, and prior to that baptism the parents were instructed in the
vows that they were to assume in this sacrament.[48]

In his 1756 treatise, Wesley wrote: "By baptism we are admitted
into the Church and consequently made members of Christ." Thus,
baptism is a prerequisite for membership in the Methodist Church.
Children who have been baptized are looked upon as "preparatory
members" under the church's care and supervision. Methodist ministers were given the responsibility of organizing the children into
classes to assure that they were instructed in the obligations of baptism and the truths of scripture.[49]

Nothing related to the theology of emergency or conditional
baptism as found in the Church of England was incorporated into the
doctrine of the Methodist Church. Likewise, there is no mention of
sponsors at baptism. In 1784, when John Wesley sent his instructions
to the Methodist Church in America, he did not mention confirmation.

Prior to the Revolutionary War all of the early Methodist ministers
who came to the colonies were itinerants; they were not ordained, and
thus could not baptize children. This situation posed any number of
problems for early adherents to this faith. Because of the close ties between early Methodism and the Anglican Church, the obvious solution was to have Anglican ministers baptize infants and administer
communion. In places such as New York City and Philadelphia, Anglican clergy did administer the sacraments for Methodists. The Anglican clerics' abandonment of their churches during the
Revolutionary War meant that there was no administration of the sac-

raments for those Methodists and Anglicans who chose to remain in Pennsylvania. In fact, the administration of the sacraments was the one issue that forced John Wesley into his decision to establish the Methodist Church in America.

St. George's Methodist Church in Philadelphia was founded in 1769 but its registers do not begin until 1785. A typical entry from the post-1785 St. George's register lists the date of baptism, the name of the infant, the names of both parents, and the date of birth. Most of the pre-Revolutionary War baptisms for members of St. George's were performed by Rev. William Stringer, pastor of St. Paul's Episcopal Church in Philadelphia. Accordingly, if ever a record for St. Paul's can be found, then baptisms for early members of the Methodist Church will possibly be found in that register.

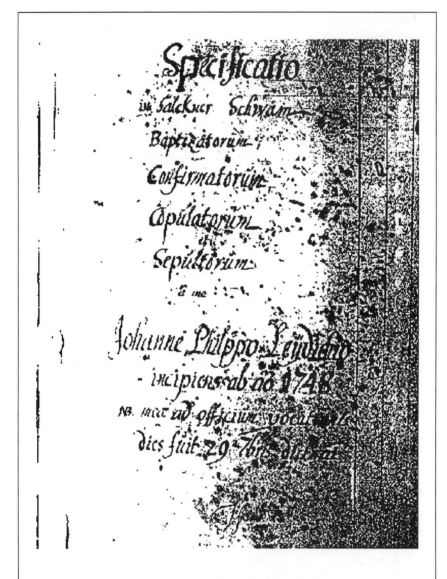

Title page for the church record of
Falckner Swamp Reformed Church, Montgomery County,
initiated by Rev. Johan Philipp Leydich in 1748.

Chapter 5

The Reformed Position

Reformed, a term dating from the sixteenth century, embodies a theological position established by Ulrich Zwingli (1484–1531) and John Calvin (1509–1564), and as a generic expression it represents several denominations identified as being of the reformed tradition. Those churches include the German Reformed Church, the Swiss Reformed Church, the Dutch Reformed Church, and the Presbyterian Church.

The founders of reformed doctrine, Calvin and Zwingli, were more radical than Martin Luther in their ideas and more systematic in their approach to changing the church. The denominations these two men helped to establish organized around pastors, teachers, elders, and deacons. Episcopal ordination and bishops were out. With regard to baptism, their break from orthodox Catholic traditions was fairly complete.

The Presbyterians

The foundations of Presbyterian theology are based on the ideas of John Calvin, who retained the traditional position that baptism was entrance into the church. In Calvin's scheme, baptism was a seal or sign of God's covenant of grace for believers and their children. As a sign it proclaimed God's forgiveness and redemption in Jesus Christ.[1]

In Calvin's view, salvation arises from the sacrificial death of the Son of God. The washing of water in baptism symbolizes the washing of Christ's blood, for "[i]n baptism, God washes us by the blood of his Son and regenerates us by his spirit. . . ."[2] John Calvin believed that this saving spirit of God also saved infants who died unbaptized.[3]

Calvin rejected the traditional concept that baptism constitutes automatic salvation; in other words, baptism does not guarantee salvation. According to Calvin, some who were baptized would be lost and some would be saved. "God's justice demands the damnation of most men. God had determined both whom he would admit to salvation and who he would condemn to destruction."[4] Calvin interpreted Ephesians 1: 3–7 to mean that this determination was made by God long before the creation.[5]

Martin Luther had earlier introduced the element of faith into the theology of baptism, maintaining the view that what brought man to baptism was faith. This presence of faith in a newborn was a difficult concept for many theologians, including John Calvin, to accept. Calvin formulated a philosophy under which the faith of a child was of no consequence—it was the faith of the parents that brought the infant to baptism.[6]

John Calvin totally rejected the Catholic idea of spiritual kinship and godparents.[7] Because it was parents' faith that brought a child to baptism, the parents took responsibility for the spiritual welfare of their children and made the vows to bring them up in the church. An integral part of the baptismal service was a congregational vow to help nurture, support, and aid the parents in developing the spiritual life of the infant. Thus, similar to Moravian baptisms, Presbyterian baptisms were performed in the presence of the congregation; private baptisms as practiced by the Lutherans and Catholics were rare. If private baptism became necessary, an elder of the church was present to symbolically represent the congregation and make the vows on their behalf.[8]

Eligibility for the Presbyterian rite of baptism was based on membership in the church. The Presbytery of Donegal in Lancaster County, Pennsylvania, "ordered that only those who are regular members of their respective congregations and contribute their share of public expenses in said Congregation were entitled to certificates of membership. An individual who did not possess such a certificate of membership was deprived of the priviledges of sealing ordinances," defined as baptism and communion.[9] But membership was not the sole requirement. One or both parents also had to be in good standing in the church as is evidenced by an entry found in the records of the Forks of the Brandywine Presbyterian Church in Chester County, Pennsylvania. On 16 June 1768 the son of William and Jean Temple was baptized. The minister noted in the record that the child was baptized "on account of the mother," and that the father was under censure.[10]

The Presbyterian Church retained the concept of confirmation—the acceptance of responsibility for a spiritual life at an accountable age. Presbyterians, however, rejected the process and the terminology used by the Catholics and other denominations. After proper preparation and an examination, children baptized into the church as infants were encouraged to make a public profession of their faith when they reached the age of accountability.[11]

John Calvin's belief that children who die unbaptized were saved by the spirit of God mitigated the urgency of baptism. In this light, it should not be too surprising that he also rejected both emergency baptism and conditional baptism. Calvin considered emergency baptism to be a gross exaggeration of the sacrament and an intrusion upon the office of the minister.[12]

According to Calvin's philosophy, the church had the right to regulate all details of faith, worship, and morals.[13] In eighteenth-century Pennsylvania, the Presbyterians regulated their churches and controlled access to the sacraments, which were called sealing ordinances. Attendance at worship and the observance of the scaraments was not only a duty but a privilege, and anyone guilty of behavior unbecoming a member of the church was in danger of having his/her right to the sacraments denied.[14]

The vehicle for control was the "session," which consisted of the pastor and church elders. The session operated much like a court, calling witnesses and ruling on the guilt or innocence of the accused. In eighteenth-century Pennsylvania, parents seeking baptism for their children in a Presbyterian Church did not merely approach the minister and request the rite. Evidence suggests that many parents also had to appear before the session. The procedure used by the Tinicum Presbyterian Church in Bucks County offers an interesting example: In 1789 that congregation adopted the rule that any person wanting the Ordinance of Baptism for himself or for his children had to announce his intention before the congregation from the pulpit of the church immediately following a service. During the following week, church members were given the opportunity to object for cause; if no objections were raised the minister could proceed with the baptism.[15]

Session records for the Tinicum Presbyterian Church show that applications for baptism were granted most of the time, but some parents were denied access to the sacrament. One gentleman, Jacob Debelt, applied for baptism for his child on 10 January 1790. On 14 February 1790 his application was denied by the session because of his ignorance—presumably of spiritual matters. On 17 April 1791, Daniel Neil applied for baptism for his son. About a month later, on 15 May 1791, Daniel Neil and his wife were called before the session to "acknowledge their faults in the sin of fornication and profess their sorrow and repentence before the congregation." After the session the child was baptized and given the name Tilyer.[16]

Another interesting example can be found in the session records of the Oxford Presbyterian Church in Chester County. On 29 May 1763, Samuel Warnock came before the session to seek baptism for his child. According to the session records Warnock's style of life and coversation were offensive. Warnock acknowledged that if he had given offense he was sorry, and he promised to amend his ways in the future. The session granted the baptism.[17]

Baptismal records for Presbyterian churches in Pennsylvania are not plentiful. Evidence confirms that at least twelve Presbyterian congregations were established in the the counties of Bucks, Philadelphia, Montgomery, Northampton, Chester, and Delaware before 1760. Only three registers for those congregations can be found: Abington Presbyterian in Montgomery County, and the First and Second Presbyterian churches in the city of Philadelphia.

Information taken from the minutes of the Presbyterian Church Synod suggests that early records for the remaining congregations were not lost; they were probably never kept. In 1766, the synod decided that "registers of births, baptisms, marriages and burials are to be regularly kept in each congregation."[18] This decision implies that careful attention to record-keeping had not been an earlier priority. After 1766, more baptismal registers for Presbyterian churches can be found. Records for the Tinicum Presbyterian Church in Bucks County begin in 1769, and the register for the Newtown Presbyterian Church in the same county begins in 1771. In Philadelphia, the Second Presbyterian Church was organized in 1743 but did not begin officially keeping records until 1769.

The experience of Rev. John Carmichael, pastor of the Forks of the Brandywine Presbyterian Church in Chester County, was probably typical. On 1 June 1768, he wrote the following: "In as much as there hath not been kept a regular register of the children which hath been baptized in this congregation of the Forks of the Brandywine since my settlement in this place [in 1761] as their minister altho. there hath been a great number baptized every year this being a very numerous flourishing congregation and seeing the keeping such a register is useful in itself and it is now enjoyned or recommended by the Rvd Synod I shall now endeavor to record in this book a true account of those baptized by me hereafter in this congregation which are as followeth since the synod May 1768."[19]

Unfortunately, Rev. Carmichael was terribly inconsistent with his record-keeping. He maintained the baptismal register for four years only—that is, the register begins in 1768 and runs until 1772. Other records indicate that Rev. Carmichael, who died in 1786, was the pastor of this congregation for another fourteen years. Any records that he may have kept beyond 1772 have never been found.[20]

A similar pattern of sloppy or incomplete record-keeping can be found in other church records as well. The Tinicum Presbyterian session records begin in 1769, then end abruptly in 1773; they do not resume until 1788. A copy of the entries illustrating this obvious hiatus appears on the following page. The Tinicum church was not unique. Others also neglected to keep complete records, including the Newtown Presbyterian Church in Bucks County, initiated in 1771, for which baptismal records were maintained for the first year only, then resume in 1782.[21]

In the absence of baptismal registers, genealogists working on

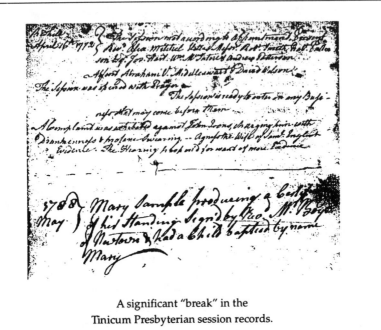

A significant "break" in the
Tinicum Presbyterian session records.

Presbyterian families should use session records as an alternative
source. Session records are not baptismal records—that is, they do not
always furnish dates of birth and/or baptism—but these records frequently designate relationships. The session records of the Tinicum
Presbyterian Church in Bucks County offer a good example, providing the names of any number of fathers who petitioned the session for
the Ordinance of Baptism. Dates of session meetings are provided,
and frequently the name of the child is recorded.

Generally speaking, Presbyterian baptismal records are fairly simple and straightforward. Usually the minister recorded the name of
the infant, the name of the father, and the date of baptism. Variations,
however, can be found. Rev. Jedediah Andrews recorded the date of
baptism, the name of the infant, the names of both parents and, occasionally, the date of birth.[22] Similarly, the minister of the Faggs Manor
Presbyterian Church in Chester County left a record of baptisms
wherein he recorded the name of the infant, date of baptism and—
again—the names of both parents.

In some unusual cases, Presbyterian records note details relating to the circumstances of certain baptisms. Two examples of these kinds of entries, both dated 1769, appear on a single page of the register for the Tinicum Presbyterian Church in Bucks County:

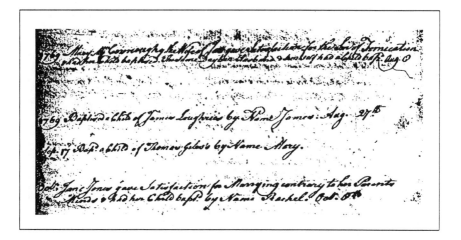

In the first case, Mary Mc Connoughy "gave Satisfaction for the Sin of Fornication"; in the second, "Jane Jones gave Satisfaction for Marrying contrary to her Parents Minds."[23] Note that, in the latter example, the child is named but neither the date of birth nor the father's name is given.

The Reformed Church

In eighteenth-century Pennsylvania, the term "Reformed Church" generally meant the German Reformed Church, whose membership included both Swiss and German immigrants. The Reformed Church in those two countries shared a similarity of belief. Unlike the Presbyterians and the Lutherans, the beliefs of the Reformed Church were not founded on the doctrines of any one person; Reformed Church theology was based on the thoughts and conclusions of several men, including Ulrich Zwingli, John Calvin, Philip Melanchthon (1497–1560), and Heinrich Bullinger (1504–1575).[24]

The Heidelberg Catechism is the single most important document that expresses the doctrine of the Reformed Church. This catechism,

written in 1563 by Zacharius Ursinus (1534–1583) and Casper Ole-
vanius (1536–1587) at the request of Elector Frederick III (1515–1576),
the first German Prince to accept Reformed beliefs, became the em-
bodiment of the church's religious views.[25]

The Heidelberg Catechism does not discuss the miraculous salvation conferred by baptism as found in Catholic and Anglican church
doctrine. Ulrich Zwingli held the opinion that "[t]he sacraments were
not miraculous vehicles but symbols of divine grace."[26] According to
the catechism, baptism in the Reformed Church is a visible Holy sign
or seal of God's promise of the salvation that comes through Christ's
sacrifice. The washing of water in baptism is an external sign of the in-
ternal washing of sin by Christ's blood.[27]

According to Reformed Church doctrine, infants are the proper
subjects of baptism for "they as well as adults are included in the
Covenant and the Church of God . . . [and] redemption is promised to
them no less than to an adult."[28] Like the Presbyterian Church, the Reformed Church limited baptism to children or infants of communicant
members; one or both parents had to have received confirmation in
the church. Traditionally the church could deny baptism to infants
whose parents were not church members unless one of the parents expressed a sincere desire for admission to communion.[29]

Many of the ideas about baptism expressed in the Heidelberg Catechism are similar to those found in Presbyterian church doctrine. One
area wherein these two churches differed was the subject of predestination. Presbyterian doctrine is strictly Calvinistic in its creed, accept-
ing the view that some who are baptized will be lost. The German
Reformed Church is more open on this issue, never having adopted a
rigorously rigid position on predestination.[30]

The early Presbyterian and Reformed churches also diverged in
the implementation of other aspects of their theology. In Reformed
practice, parents with children of questionable birth did not have to
publicly humiliate themselves before the session or congregation. A
parent seeking baptism for an illegitimate child in the Reformed
church probably made a private confession before the minister; after
the infant was baptized, the minister noted in the record that the child
was born illegitimate.

In 1747 four ministers of the German Reformed Church and lay

representatives from nineteen congregations met to organize a governing body for the church in Pennsylvania. This group was named
Coetus. Evidence from the records of their meetings shows that limitations were placed on baptismal practice. At the second meeting of
the Coetus in September 1748 the question arose as to whether a Reformed minister belonging to the Coetus could dispense communion
and baptize infants under the care or charge of another member of the
Coetus. It was decided that ". . . no minister shall admit to communion
any members of the Reformed Congregations whether husband or
wife or single person who formerly went to Communion to another
minister belonging to the Coetus, without the former minister's
knowledge, and unless a certificate be shown. The same regulation
shall hold for Holy Baptism as for Holy Supper. Cases of necessity, in

A portion of a page from baptismal records of the
First Reformed Church, Philadelphia.

which one brother feels duty bound to help the other are expected. The minister who is so requested shall take no fee for his labor but shall perform it as for his brother and therefore he shall give a baptismal certificate to those caring for the baptized child and shall enjoin upon them to give this certificate to their regular minister."[31] Additional limitations on baptism were instituted at the 11 April 1755 meeting of the Coetus, where a resolution was adopted stating that ". . . Holy Baptism shall not be administered to a stranger except in case of necessity."[32]

Ulrich Zwingli shared John Calvin's view that all children who die in infancy are saved, even if unbaptized. Zwingli felt that children were too young to sin.[33] The Reformed Church, like the Presbyterian Church, did not include emergency or conditional baptism in its practice, and the church did not alter its position in Pennsylvania on emergency baptism, as is evidenced by a 1773 decision of Coetus, wherein Caspar Wack (1752–1839), a Reformed minister, informed the governing body that a schoolmaster had "dared to baptize a child. Asked for an opinion, the Coetus declared that such a baptism was invalid."[34]

Witnesses shared in the baptismal rite as practiced by the Reformed Church. The Reformed Constitution of 1748 stated that "besides parents witnesses shall be present at the baptism, and this well established custom shall not be lightly changed."[35] Restrictions were placed on the qualification of anyone called to serve as a witness. The 1748 constitution also specifically stated that witnesses to the baptism were to be "chosen persons who have confessed the pure doctrine of the Gospel and whose lives are blameless."[36] A later constitution stated that the parents were to respond to the questions and were to assume the obligation of nurturing the child in the church.[37]

In working with transcriptions or translations of Reformed Church registers in Pennsylvania, researchers will find the words "sponsor" and "witness" used interchangeably. This confusion probably results from the German to English translation of the word *taufzeugen*. The translator or transcriber undoubtedly confused the German word for witness with his or her conception of the third-party role at baptisms. Witness and sponsor have different meanings. Traditionally, baptismal sponsors answer for the child while witnesses of a baptism merely attest to the fact that the baptism took place. Contrary to technically correct definitions, parents having their children baptized according to Reformed tradition took the vows and the "sponsors" served only as the witnesses.

The reason that baptism in the Reformed Church was limited to infants of parents who were communicant members, or to one or both parents who promised to become communicant member, obviously relates to the issue of sponsors. Any parent promising to God in the presence of the congregation to raise the infant in thc church would, almost of necessity, have to be a communicant member of the church in order to fulfill that obligation.

Confirmation as practiced by the Reformed Church does not include anointing with oil or conferring of the Holy Spirit. Rather, confirmation is a profession of faith. Young people who are baptized into the church as infants are instructed in the beliefs of the church, and that instruction is supervised by the both the pastor and church elders. Upon completion of study, candidates are examined to assure that they understand the fundamental doctrines of the Christian faith. The candidates are then admitted as communicant members after making their "profession of faith."[38]

Reformed ministers generally recorded in the church register the name of the infant, the names of both parents, the dates of birth and baptism, and names of the witnesses. Variations on this format can be found in Reformed records, and frequently those variations will reflect the style of the minister. Rev. Friedrich S. Rothenbueler (1726–1766), for example, in the two years he was pastor of the First Reformed Church in Philadelphia, also recorded in the baptismal register of that church the places of origin in Germany and Switzerland for seventy-three of his parishioners.[39]

Because Reformed baptismal records are similar to Lutheran records, someone working with both denominations might assume they shared similar beliefs on baptism—a mistake, to be sure, for they do not.

The Dutch Reformed Church

Several early Dutch Reformed congregations were established in Bucks and Monroe counties of Pennsylvania. These congregations had ties with the Dutch Reformed Church in New York and their records can be considered evidence of a migration from New York into eastern Pennsylvania.

The Dutch Reformed Church was the first denomination from the Reformed tradition established in American Colonies. The first Dutch Reformed pastor came to New York in 1628 to help organize the church and to administer the sacraments.[40] This denomination, following the theology of John Calvin, is similar to Presbyterianism in terms of its doctrine and beliefs on baptism.[41] A shared theology helps to explain the rapport that existed between the early Dutch Reformed churches in Pennsylvania and nearby Presbyterian churches. A good example of these close ties can be found in the role of Rev. Jonathan DuBois (1727–1772), minister of the Low Dutch Reformed Church in Southampton Township, Bucks County, who also served as the pastor of the Abington Presyterian Church in Montgomery County.[42] Further early-nineteenth-century evidence is apparent in the fact that, prompted by a dwindling membership, the Reformed Dutch Church in Smithfield Township in Monroe County, Pennsylvania, reorganized and combined with the nearby Presbyterian Church.[43]

A typical entry in a Dutch Reformed baptismal register furnishes the name of the minister, the date of baptism, the names of the parents, and the names of the witnesses if any were present. Genealogical researchers should note that eighteenth-century Dutch Reformed practices differed from those of the Presbyterians in that the names of witnesses for their (Dutch Reformed) baptisms were frequently recorded in the registers.[44] Dates of birth, however, were rarely provided.[45]

Dutch Reformed baptismal records are very consistent; in fact, the consistency of these records is a particularly striking feature. This uniformity is indicative of the status the Dutch Reformed Church had in Holland—that is, in 1588 this Church became the established state church of Holland.[46] The consistency of baptismal entries in Dutch Reformed church registers suggests that laws in Holland, similar to those passed in the 1603 act of the British Parliament, may have mandated the information that was to be included in baptismal records.

Family historians working with Dutch Reformed baptismal registers must exercise extreme caution. The Holland Dutch used an ancient naming system called "patronymics," wherein a child took his father's first name as his second name. The second name was not fixed; rather, it changed with each generation. The adoption of fixed surnames in Pennsylvania and New York by these early Dutch families may have taken place gradually. Thus, genealogists working on these families may have to track both a fixed and a patronymic name.

Within a patromymic naming system, women retain their birth surnames instead of adopting that of their husbands. The maiden surnames of the mothers of the infants as recorded in the Dutch Reformed registers in Pennsylvania and New York suggest that this pattern continued in New York and Pennsylvania. The baptismal record for Arie Brinck as found in the rgister of the Dutch Reformed Church in Lower Smithfield Township, Monroe County, Pennsylvania, is typical: Arie, child of Lambart Brinck and Rachel van Garden, was baptized 25 April 1744; witnesses were Daniel Broadhead and Hester Luykese, his wife.[47] Notice that the baptized child's mother did not take her husband's surname; similarly, the surname of the female witness does not match that of her husband. Women such as Rachel van Garden and Hester Luykese—as well as other women of Dutch Reformed faith in eighteenth-century Pennsylvania and New York— were identified throughout their lives by their birth names. Because these women did not take the surnames of their husbands, genealogists searching for parents of their female ancestors with a Dutch Reformed background will have to search both fixed and patronymic names.

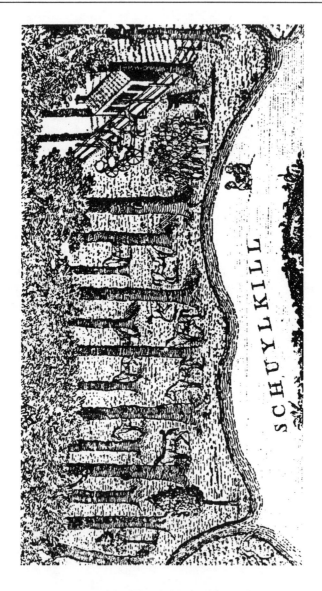

"Baptism on the Schuylkill" (engraving, 1770).
From *City of Independence: Views of Philadelphia Before 1800*, 84.

Chapter 6

Anabaptist and Baptist Traditions

Once Martin Luther introduced the element of faith into his theology of baptism, it was inevitable that others would ask the question: "How can an infant have faith?" Thomas Munzer (1489?–1525), Menno Simons (1496–1561), John Smythe (1570–1612), Ernst Christoph Hochmann von Hochenau (1670–1721), and others asked that very question, indeed, and the answers they arrived at became the basis for the Anabaptist and Baptist faiths.

Several religious groups in eighteenth-century Pennsylvania practiced of these new traditions. Among them were the Mennonites, Amish, Baptists, Dunkards, Seventh-Day Adventists, and the followers of Conrad Beissel (1690–1768), who established a celibate community at Ephrata, Pennsylvania. The only ritual that adherents of these traditions held in common was their doctrine of "believer baptism"— that is, a form of baptism freely entered into by a believing adult. But these faiths disagreed on many issues, not the least of which was the technique used to administer baptism. Mennonites baptized their members by affusion (pouring).[1] Baptists baptized by immersion backwards,[2] while the Dunkards baptized their followers by immersion three times forward in a flowing stream.[3]

Genealogists will experience significant difficulty in trying to find records for followers of these faiths for several reasons. First and foremost, the persecution each of these groups suffered was an enormous disincentive to maintaining records. In 1648, as a matter of fact, the English House of Commons passed a bill that punished opponents of infant baptism with life imprisonment.[4]

Second, the differences in basic theology also presented a problem; consequently, the doctrine of "believer baptism" diminished the value of baptismal records because baptism was an activity no longer associated with birth. The value of baptismal records for genealogical research was, of course, never a consideration.

The Mennonites

Anabaptism first appeared in Switzerland in 1524 among the Swiss Brethren, who immediately came into conflict with Ulrich Zwingli, the Swiss reformer, over their insistence that infant baptism was meaningless and should be repeated in maturity. The theology and practices of the Anabaptists were very unsettling to a culture that for centuries had been ingrained with a traditional belief that the rite of baptism left an indelible mark on the soul and was performed only once. So established where these ideas that shortly after the first Anabaptist congregation was formed in Zurich, its followers were fined then jailed, and after 1526, drowned.[5]

Anabaptism spread to southern Germany, to Austria, and to other parts of Switzerland—and just as quickly as it spread, efforts were made to supress it. The little duchy of Swabia reported in 1528 that 500 to 1000 horseman went out into the country to "kill Taufers like wild beasts and take their property."[6] In 1529, the Diet of Speyer passed a law under which all adult Anabaptists were to be condemned to death without trial.[7]

In the 1530s, Menno Simons organized fragments of the Anabaptist movement in the Netherlands and East Friesland into congregations who later became known as Mennonites. Mennonites comprised the largest group of Anabaptists to settle in Pennsylvania.

Mennonites practice "believer baptism." For Mennonites and others in the Anabaptist tradition, the coupling of baptism and repentence as found in the New Testament is "proof" that baptism could not be administered to anyone but a true believer. To followers of the Mennonite religious faith, baptism is a rite that has no significance for infants because repentence must precede baptism; they see infant baptism as a washing of water without meaning.[8]

Mennonites also object the the coercive nature of infant baptism. The church, according to Mennonites, is a voluntary association of those who have both experienced a personal enlightenment or conversion, and have reached a decision—based on a personal belief—to accept Christ and to enter into His church. If baptism is to be an initiation rite into the church, then it must be entered into freely. Because infants cannot be involved in the decision regarding their own baptism, they are being brought into the church by a means other than personal choice.[9]

The standard mode for administering the sacrament of baptism among most Mennonites is pouring. In 1718 in Pennsylvania, at a typical Mennonite baptism, "The person to be baptized being an adult kneels; a preacher holds his hands over him or her while the deacon pours water into the hands of the preacher, which runs on the head of the person to be baptized after which prayer accompanied by the imposition of hands closes the ceremony."[10]

The history of record-keeping for Anabaptists in Euorpe is varied—that is, records can be found in some areas but not in others. The pattern of keeping records mirrors, in some ways, the repression Mennonites and other Anabaptists suffered throughout Europe. The Dutch were the first to achieve some modicum of religious toleration, and thus the archives of the Mennonite Church in Amsterdam have the largest collection of records. Baptismal, marriage, and children's records can be found in the Amsterdam collection.[11]

Anabaptists in Switzerland, Germany, and Austria kept no records, but, given the persecution Anabaptists suffered in these three countries, this fact should not be too surprising. After the Thirty Years' War, Mennonites settled in areas of Germany that had been depopulated during that war, and some birth, marriage, and burial records for Mennonites in the Palatinate and Hesse were included in the parish records of the state churches. The Mennonite Church in Germany did not begin keeping its own records until the nineteenth century.[12]

Mennonites in eighteenth-century Pennsylvania were of Swiss and German extraction, and in Pennsylvania they maintained the traditions of their forebearers. This means, of course, that the early Mennonites in Pennsylvania kept no records.

Woodcut from a *Taufschein*,
suggestive of the Mennonite or Amish Mennonite
mode of baptism.

(courtesy of Corinne P. Earnest)

The Amish Mennonites

Other practitioners of anabaptism were the Amish, who began their immigration into Pennsylvania in 1720. "Amish Mennonite" is the correct name for this group of anabaptists who followed the ideas of Jakob Ammann (1644–17??), a late-seventeenth-century Mennonite Bishop. Ammann withdrew from the Mennonite fellowship in 1693 because he felt that the Mennonite Church was lax in its doctrine and practice. Specifically, he insisted on the strict enforcement of the doctrine of *Meidung*, otherwise known as shunning, a practice whereby the Amish avoid all social interaction with any person put "under the ban."[13] Another change Jakob Ammann made to the order of worship was the introduction of foot washing as an ordinace of the Amish church, a custom that was not practiced by other Swiss Anabaptists.[14]

The Amish Mennonites represented a conservative point of view and were very rigid in the practice of their faith. They insisted upon sharp discipline and an inflexibile adherence to practices they considered essential to a true Christian Church. It was ". . . this inflexible conservatism [that] has marked the Amish ever since and which has resulted in an unchanging perpetuation of forms of worship and church organization as well as costume, customs and language. To this day, Old Order Amish in North America have continued with little change the Amish way as fixed by Jakob Ammann and his associates in the year 1700."[15]

In the traditions of anabaptism, the Amish practice "believer baptism," that is, baptism entered into freely by a believing adult. Baptism, as seen by the Amish, is entrance into the church and is believed to be the sign of a mature decision on the part of the recipient to follow Christ.[16]

Details related to the rite of baptism varied from one Amish group to another. Dress was important. Young girls who were candidates for baptism, for example, wore black ribbons in their net caps as opposed to the usual white. A young man generally wore a dark blue coat, a white shirt, and a black tie. At an Amish baptism, the bishop who performed the rite asked a series of questions of each supplicant and offered prayer. The candidates for baptism kneeled and a deacon

> . . . came forward with a pail of water, and a cup and stood at the
> right hand of the Bishop. The two men approached the first

young man . . . [and] the Bishop placed his hands on the boy's head and said, "Upon the confession of your faith, repenting and grieving your sin, you are baptized with water in the name of the Father, Son, and Holy Ghost," When he said the word baptized he cupped his hands and the deacon poured a small amount of water into them. The Bishop released it onto the boy's head. . . . [He then] repeated the process for the remaining boys. When the pair came to the first girl, the [deacon and bishop] were joined by their wives. The deacon's wife removed the first girl's cap. She handed it to the bishop's wife [who] replaced each girl's cap after the water had been poured.

When the last girl was baptized, the bishop returned to the first boy, who like the other was still kneeling. He grasped his right hand and said "In the name of the congregation I offer you my hand; arise to a new beginning. May the Lord transform you from your sinful condition into the righteousness of his kingdom. Be therefore welcome as a brother in the congregation."[17]

The Amish kept no eighteenth-century baptismal records.

The Baptists

In the late sixteenth century in England, groups of separatists abandoned their earlier efforts to reform or purify the established church and sought separation. Among those early groups were the Puritans who, in 1620, settled in Massachusetts. Another group of separatists was founded by John Smythe, who in 1608 became convinced that the logical way to separate from the established church was to renounce infant baptism, the rite of initiation into the church. Smythe equated infant baptism with spiritual adultery. He wanted to establish a church of true believers where baptism was awarded only to those who professed the true faith and who understood its significance. He rebaptized himself by pouring, and then baptized many of his followers.[18]

A year later, in 1609, John Smythe along with Thomas Helwys (ca. 1570–1616) founded the first Baptist Church in England. Smythe held the view that ". . . man has the freedom to believe in Christ; that whomever will believe may be saved . . . ."[19] Smythe rejected John

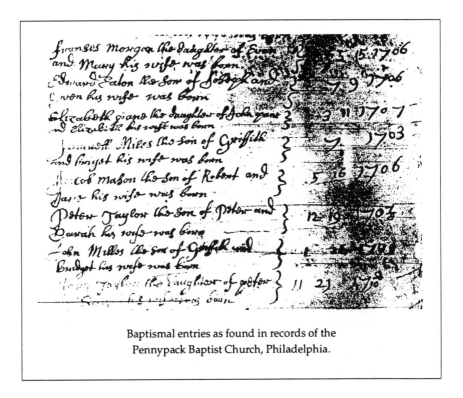

Baptismal entries as found in records of the
Pennypack Baptist Church, Philadelphia.

Calvin's theology of predestination and, because of this position, he and his followers became know as General Baptists.

Another group of Baptists were identified as Particular Baptists. This group did not separate from the General Baptists but, rather, sprang up independently. Particular Baptists adopted John Calvin's ideas on predestination and limited atonement. Like the General Baptists, the Particular Baptists concluded that baptism applied only to believers and not to infants.[20]

In the 1640s the Particular Baptists adopted backward immersion as their mode of baptism because, among other things, it was the method used by the early church. The mode of baptism held great significance for Particular Baptists, who believed that immersion resembled burial and rising again. According to their theology, the rite of baptism demonstrated that we are dead and buried with Christ and that we have risen to a regenerated life. "In immersion a man is covered over as if he were in his grave; there can be no breathing except for a second, as if man were dead; he rises out of the water as if he were ascending from his grave."[21]

Baptism was not the only issue separating the Baptists from other churches in seventeenth-century England. Baptists, both General and Particular, strongly believed in the separation of church and state, freedom of religion and in a congregational form of church government.[22]

The first Baptist Church in Pennsylvania was founded in 1684 by Thomas Dungan, who had come to Bucks County, Pennsylvania, from New England, where the original Baptist churches in the American Colonies had been established. After Dungan returned to New England, this early Bucks County church died out.[23]

In 1688, the Pennypack Baptist Church was founded in Philadelphia by Elias Keach, a Particular Baptist. Keach's following was scattered throughout southeastern Pennsylvania, necessitating the formation of separate groups who joined together to hold quarterly and annual meetings. Baptists churches that descended from the Pennypack Baptist Church include Brandywine (Chester County), Southampton (Bucks County), and Hopewell (New Jersey).[24]

An early extant baptismal register for the Pennypack Baptist Church was probably kept in part by Elias Keach. Most of the entries in this record list the names of church members along with their dates of baptism. Keach and later Baptist ministers listed approximately one hundred entries in this record, providing dates of birth and names of parents for the Pennypack church members. Many of these entries used the Quaker method for recording dates in numeric form: "born 15 2nd month 1689," "baptized 4 mo 1 day 1704," etc.[25]

The First Baptist Church in Philadelphia was established in 1762. Organizers of this church were Keithian Baptists or Quakers who independently adopted Baptist doctrine. A register for this congregation lists names of members along with dates of birth, names of parents, and, for women, frequently the mother's maiden name.[26]

The records for the Pennypack and First Baptist Churches are aberrations in that Baptist registers, where they exist, seldom list dates of birth or names of parents.

The Dunkards

In 1708, almost one hundred years after John Smythe established the Baptist Church in England, a group of German Pietists lead by Alexander Mack baptized themselves in the Eder River at Schwarzenau in the county of Wittgenstein in Germany and formed a covenant to live in all things according to the New Testament. They referred to one another as "Brethren."[27]

Alexander Mack and his fellow Brethren based their beliefs on those of Ernst Christoph Hochmann von Hochenau, a German Pietist who taught that infant baptism had no basis in scripture. Hochmann held the view that baptism should be administered only if and when the recipient had a God-given conviction sufficient enough to withstand the tests of the suffering that would inevitably come to those who held baptist beliefs.[28]

Furthermore, Mack, in one of his tracts on baptism, argued that a child did not suffer damnation if he or she died unbaptized because the baptismal command was directed to adults rather than to children. Thus, even children of believing adults had to wait for baptism until they were moved by the Holy Spirit into expressing a desire for baptism. Within Dunkard baptismal practice, the rite does not affect or guarantee the work of God and no regeneration or miraculous salvation results from its practice in the Brethren's concept of baptism. Baptism, according to Dunkard doctrine, was commanded by God and it was seen as an act of obedience on the part of the true believer.[29]

Gottfried Arnold (1666–1714) was another radical German Pietist who influenced the early Dunkards. Arnold, who is looked upon as the father of modern church history, thoroughly explored the history of the early church and its practices. From Arnold's history the Brethren learned that the early form of baptism was trine immersion, which prompted them to adopt this mode. At a Dunkard baptism the applicant after a public confession of faith was immersed forward three times in a flowing stream.[30]

Confirmation, looked upon as the second rite of initiation into the church, was not a part of Dunkard ritual because the church did not practice infant baptism. The Brethren adopted the early church practice of the laying on of hands after baptism. Other early church procedures embraced by the Brethren were the washing of feet and the *agape*, or Love Feast.[31]

From 1719 until 1735 almost all of the German Brethren emmi-
grated from Germany to Pennsylvania. The first group arrived in 1719
and settled in Germantown, where they established their first congregation. A second group arrived on the ship *Allen* in September of 1729.
By 1735 Dunkards had established in Pennsylvania congregations in
Germantown, Coventry (Chester County), Conestoga (Lancaster
County), and Oley and Great Swamp (both in Berks County).[32]

The Dunkard Brethren in Pennsylvania kept no baptismal records
in the eighteenth century.

Chapter 7

The Religious Society of Friends

George Fox (1624–1691) rejected the sacrament of baptism as practiced by most other churches. He believed in an inward baptism of the Holy Spirit. The external washing of baptism was seen as a meaningless outward manifestation without consequence. Fox held the conviction that outward forms and ceremonies belonged to the old Jewish Covenant, and that Jesus came to initiate a New Covenant unencumbered by ritual ceremony and symbolism. The figure of Christ, as viewed by Fox and his followers, superseded the old law and practices and opened a new approach to God. Quaker evidence that baptism was not a prerequisite for entrance into heaven can be found in Christ's remarks (Luke 23: 43) to the thief who was crucified beside him: "I say to you, today you will be with me in paradise."[1]

At the core of Religious Society of Friends (Quaker) doctrine is George Fox's theology of the "Inner Light," which held that an emanation of divine goodness and virtue passed from Jesus Christ into every human soul.[2] Quakers believed that this inner light brought the means of salvation within reach of everyone who was awakened to its existence. The Friends' idea of salvation rejected John Calvin's idea of limited atonement. Accordingly, Christ did not die for a chosen few but for all mankind.[3]

The sacraments were not the only practices of the other Christian denominations rejected by the Friends. They also rejected ordination, churches, and ministers; they condemned what they called "hireling clergy" and "steeple house ways." In place of ministers, Quakers substituted lay missionaries and exhorters.[4]

The organizational structure of the Religious Society of Friends differed radically from other denominations as well. The Quakers organized around a system of "Meetings," all of which kept records. The Preparative Meeting was at the bottom of the structure. Worship sessions at this level were held each First Day (Sunday) and mid-week, in the meetinghouse built by the Preparative Meeting or in individual homes. A separate Preparative Meeting for men and women was not uncommon. Entrance into the Society took place at this level—that is, this Preparative Meeting received applications for membership as well as notices of intentions to marry. The Monthly Meeting consisted of several Preparative Meetings, and most of the business activities of the Society were conducted at the Monthly Meeting level. Several Monthly Meetings came together to form a Quarterly Meeting, and the annual Yearly Meeting could include meetings from a fairly large geographic area. While the weekly worship session was held at the preparative level, worship was an integral part of all meetings.[5]

In 1656, at a gathering of several elders in Yorkshire, England, a document was approved to establish the organizational structure of the Society of Friends. Clause 8 of that document reads: "Every meeting to keep records of births, and of burials of the dead that die in the Lord."[6] This position was reiterated in a 1659 directive sent to all monthly meetings stipulating, among other things, that "all births, marriages and burials were to be recorded."[7]

The 1656 instructions were clarified by George Fox in 1669. "Let one or two [F]riends of every meeting take an account of all the marriages, births and deaths, and carry them to the Monthly [M]eetings, and let one or two there be ordered to receive them, and record them in a book, which is to be kept at the Monthly Meetings. And from thence a copy of what is recorded, is to be brought to the Quarterly Meetings, and one or Two Friends appointed there to receive them and record them in a book which is to be kept for the whole county. And this will be most safe that if one book should happen to be lost the other may be preserved for the use of such as may have occasion."[8]

George Fox's 1669 instruction implies that vital records were to be maintained by both the monthly and quarterly meetings, and suggests that genealogists may find a double set of vital records in England. No evidence for a double set of records exists in Pennsylvania. As far as can be determined, all records of births, marriages, and burials in eighteenth-century Pennsylvania were notated in the monthly meeting journals only.

Friends did not use the traditional method of recording dates. Specifically, they did not employ the months of the Gregorian calendar when recording dates of birth or burial. Dates in Friends Meeting records were written in numeric form: July 4, 1776 was written as "7th month 4 1776"or "4 7th month 1776." The Quaker method for dating of events was initiated in 1653 by George Fox, who felt that the days of the week should be identified as God titled them in the book of Genesis: first-day, second-day, third-day, etc.[9] Names of the months were not used because they were derived from the names of pagan gods.[10]

Children of Quaker-practicing parents became birthright members of the Society of Friends. Entrance by birth into the Society, at least in England, was through a ritual called "nomination" that entailed a careful selection of the child's name coupled with the registration of that name into the Meeting record. Present at the nomination to certify the record were those who had been present at the birth. William Penn, in 1694, described the custom as follows: "The parents name their own children, which is usually some days after they were born, in the presence of the midwife if she can be there, and those that were at the birth, who afterward sign a certificate, for that purpose prepared, of the birth and name of the child or children, which is recorded in the proper book in the monthly meeting to which the parents belong, avoiding the accustomed ceremonies and festivals."[11]

Nomination was probably not used in Pennsylvania. According to the process as described by William Penn, birth records for children of Quaker parents would have had to be registered in chronological order. The majority of entries in Pennsylvania's monthly meeting records, however, are in a family format; each entry lists the names of both parents along with the names and dates of birth for each of the children in the family. The only records found in Pennsylvania that hint of the Quaker nomination process are the entries for the four children of John and Mary Cresson born in Philadelphia between 1693 and 1699. Each entry lists the name of the infant, date of birth, and the names of the women present when the child was born. The same person, Ann Parsons, is identified as the midwife for all four births.[12] The page from Philadelphia Monthly Meeting records containing these entries is reproduced below:

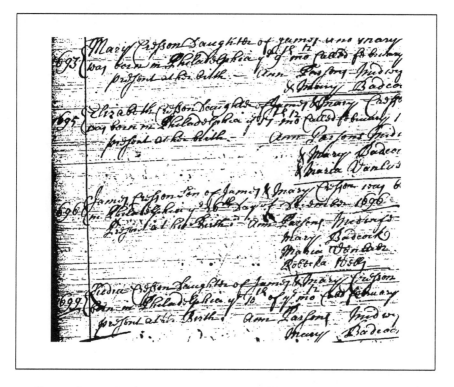

As early as the late-seventeenth century, minutes for monthly meetings in Pennsylvania show that Friends who had recently arrived in Pennsylvania were urged to record family information. The minutes of the first Meeting of the Philadelphia Friends note that on 9 11th month 1682 those present agreed ". . . that Friends of this meeting do bring their certificates from their respective meetings of Friends they belonged to and they be registered according to their time of arrival in this province. . . . It was also agreed that Friends of this city and county that have deceased since their arrival be brought in and recorded in the monthly meeting book."[13]

Minutes for the Middletown Monthly Meeting in Bucks County disclose that on the first day of the eleventh month of 1683, "it is ordered by this meeting that friends bring their births and burials."[14] The introduction to the vital records for this same meeting note ". . .an account of births of Friends children borne in England given by their parents to Cuthbert Hayhurst."[15] The Middletown Monthly Meeting records, like many other Friends meeting records, contain vital information about members pertaining to events that occurred prior to the date the meeting was established.

Friends records are essentially family registers. In most cases, all of the children, together with their dates of birth, are listed together with the names of both parents (see example of Philadelphia Monthly Meeting records on the following page). Vital records in eighteenth-century Pennsylvania were generally recorded in the Monthly Meeting registers after the birth of the last child, as evidenced by the similarity of handwriting and the spacing of entries. Thus, birth records for some families were recorded long after the birth of the first child. The fact that most family information in Quaker records was not recorded in timely order raises the question of whether the information came from some prior list or was entered from memory.

When a child was baptized by a Presbyterian, German Lutheran, or Episcopalian minister, that event was usually recorded only once. In contrast, vital records maintained for members of the Religious Society of Friends were often recorded several times. For example, Richard Thomas was recorded in the Goshen Monthly Meeting with the date of birth 30 12th month 1744. In this record Richard is identified as the son of Richard and Phebe Thomas and he is listed with his four sibilings.[16] A later entry—in the Uwchlan Monthly Meeting records— for Richard Thomas, born 30 12th month 1744, identifies Thomzin Downing as Richard's wife and lists this couple with their nine children. This Richard Thomas is obviously listed in the first of these monthly meeting records with his parents and in the second with his wife and children.[17]

Duplicate entries appear for several reasons. Friends were frequently listed as children with their parents and later as adults with

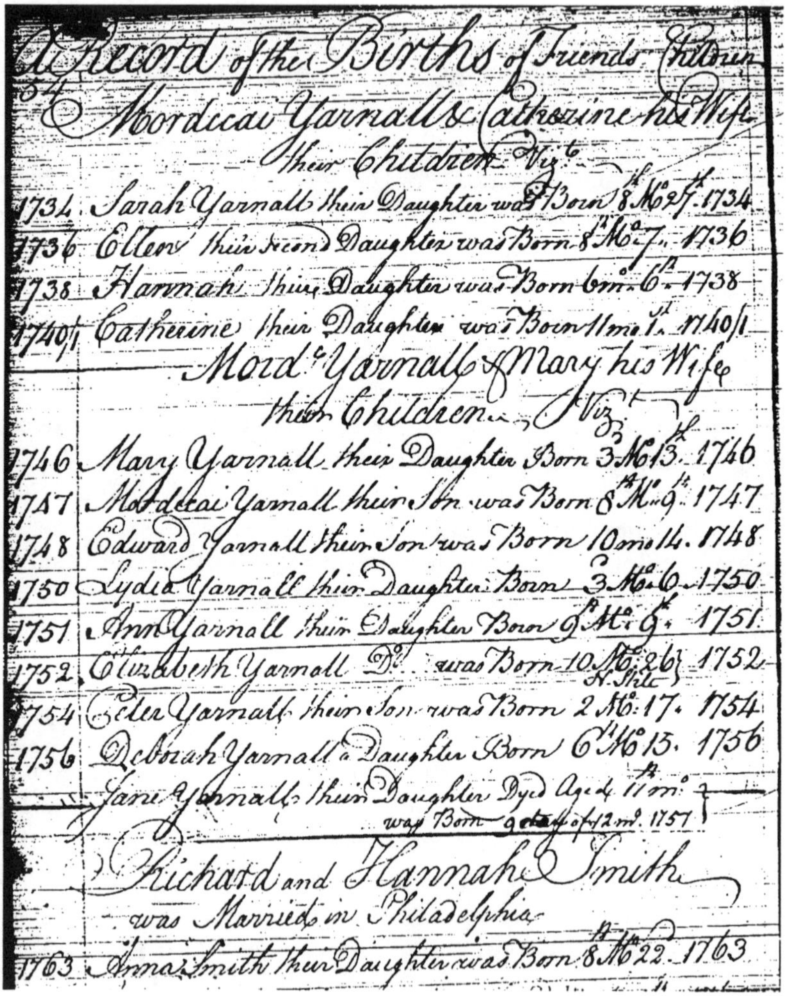

A Record of the Births of Friends Children
54 Mordecai Yarnall & Catherine his Wife
their Children Viz.
1734 Sarah Yarnall their Daughter was Born 8 Mo. 27th. 1734
1736 Ellen their second Daughter was Born 8th Mo. 7. 1736
1738 Hannah their Daughter was Born 6 mo. 6th. 1738
1740/1 Catherine their Daughter was Born 11 mo. 1st. 1740/1
Mord. Yarnall & Mary his Wife
their Children Viz.
1746 Mary Yarnall their Daughter Born 3 Mo. 13th. 1746
1747 Mordecai Yarnall their Son was Born 8th Mo. 9th. 1747
1748 Edward Yarnall their Son was Born 10 mo. 14. 1748
1750 Lydia Yarnall their Daughter Born 3 Mo. 6. 1750
1751 Ann Yarnall their Daughter Born 9th Mo. 9th. 1751
1752 Elizabeth Yarnall Do. was Born 10 Mo. 26 N. Stile 1752
1754 Peter Yarnall their Son was Born 2 Mo. 17. 1754
1756 Deborah Yarnall a Daughter Born 6th Mo. 15. 1756
Jane Yarnall their Daughter Dyed Aged 11 mo.
was Born 9th day of 12 mo. 1757
Richard and Hannah Smith
was Married in Philadelphia
1763 Anna Smith their Daughter was Born 8 Mo. 22. 1763

Family records from the Philadelphia Monthly Meeting.

their offspring as shown in the previous example. Other double entries may occur because a family moved to a new location. When they became members of another meeting their vital records were entered into a second register.

In other instances, duplicate sets of entries were generated because a meeting was "set off" from a "parent meeting" and the records were rerecorded in the new monthly meeting. Vital statistics for members of a newly-formed meeting were not copied from the prior meeting register but, rather, were begun anew with information supplied from meeting members. In 1763, for example, Pikeland and Nantmeal Preparative Meetings (Chester County) broke away from Goshen Monthly Meeting and combined to form the new Monthy Meeting of Uwchlan. At a gathering of the newly-formed Uwchlan Monthly Meeting held on 13 3rd month 1763, Thomas Milhous, Jr., was appointed to keep a regular record of births and burials and "friends are desired to furnish him with accounts thereof." Cooperation by members of the new meeting was evidently not as complete as hoped or "desired."[18] An 11 8th month 1763 report prepared by the Uwchlan Monthly Meeting and sent to the Concord Quarterly Meeting noted: "We are in the practice of keeping a record of births and burials but many particulars [members] are negligent in giving accounts."[19]

When working with Friends Meeting records, genealogists should always pay particular attention to redundant records because the second set of information may include previously unrecorded data of significant value. A classic case in point is that of Thomas and Sarah Martin, who are recorded with their children in two sets of records—the Goshen Monthly Meeting and the Uwchlan Monthly Meeting. In the Goshen records, Thomas and Sarah are listed with four children born between 1751 and 1755. The Martin family evidently joined the exodus from the Goshen Meeting in 1763 and, as members of the new meeting, provided updated information. The Uwchlan register lists Thomas and Sarah with six children, all born between 1751 and 1758. In other words, two additional children were born to this couple after 1755—information that would possibly, if not probably, have been lost if Thomas and Sarah had been as "negligent in giving accounts" as some of the other Uwchlan Meeting members. Interestingly, the later (Uwchlan) record also contains information about both Thomas Martin and his wife that is missing from the earlier (Goshen) account: Thomas Martin was born in Ireland on 21 10th month 1714. His wife Sarah, born in the 2nd month 1715, was identified as the daughter of Cadwalader and Eleanor Jones.[20] The Martin family example should convince genealogists not to assume that an older meeting has the more complete record. The reverse is certainly true in this case; a Martin descendant overlooking the second meeting record would miss invaluable data by basing family research on a single isolated account.

On the other hand, redundant records do not always provide new and interesting information; sometimes they furnish conflicting data—possibly, for example, different dates of birth. In Nottingham Meeting records, Thomas and Sarah Barnard are listed with four children: Joshua b. 6 12th month 1751; John b. 23 2nd month 1753; Ann b. 11 3rd month 1755; Hannah b. 11 12th month 1757.[21] In New Garden Meeting, this same couple is listed with eight children, but the dates of birth differ slightly from the same children listed in the Nottingham record. The New Garden records show the Barnard children as: Joshua b. 17 12th month 1751; John b. 23 2nd month 1754; Ann b. 11 3rd month 1756; Hannah b. 24 12th month 1757.[22] To find this kind of conflicting information is frustrating for the family historian but, at the same time, it evokes a cautionary watchword for all genealogical research: Skepticism. Written records are not always accurate; confirmation obtained from an alternate source is always desirable.

Genealogists working on Quaker families must also be sensitive to the movement into and out of the Religious Society of Friends. An infraction of the Society's many rules was cause for "disownment." It was easy to lose one's membership. Margaret Winn, a birthright member of the Society, was disowned by the Uwchlan Meeting on 8 6th month 1763 for her marriage by a priest to a man outside of the Society.[23] Sarah Taylor was disowned on 4 5th month 1763 by the same meeting for keeping company with men in a loose and disorderly manner at unreasonable hours of the night, and for playing cards.[24]

But Quakers did not always leave the Religious Society of Friends because of disownment. Evidence in a combination of Quaker and non-Quaker records hints that some Friends left of their own volition and sought baptism in any one of Pennsylvania's other church denominations. To illustrate, one group of entries found in a variety of sources yields a somewhat surprising set of events when assembled and compared. The Philadelphia Friends Monthly Meeting show a Mary Townsend born on 6 11th month 1747; her parents are identified as Charles and Abigail Townsend.[25] Mary Townsend's marriage to Joseph Preiss is confirmed by the will of Charles Townsend proved in Philadelphia in July of 1776.[26] The register of St. Joseph's Catholic Church in Philadelphia lists the baptism of Mary Townsend, wife of Joseph Preiss, on 13 October 1771; that same register notes the baptism of Samuel Preiss, son of Joseph Preiss and his wife Mary Townsend on 27 November 1771.[27] In other words, Mary Townsend was born to Quaker parents, left the Friends to marry and bear the child of Joseph Preiss, and received Catholic baptism as an adult at age twenty-four.

Evidence of this out-movement can be found in other records as well. A baptism for Elizabeth Creutz dated 13 August 1769 was recorded in the registers of St. Michael's and Zion Lutheran Church in Philadelphia. The pastor at the time identifies Elizabeth, the twenty-six-year-old wife of Daniel Creutz, as a Quaker. Baptized on the same day were two children of the couple: Mary, age seven, and Daniel, age three.[28] Similarly, an entry in the register of the First Presbyterian Church in Philadelphia notes, along with the baptism of Susannah Orrick on 23 August 1789, that she was the twenty-one year old daughter of William and Elizabeth Husband, Quakers.[29]

Evidence of movement out of the Society of Friends is not limited to church registers. An interesting tale about one Quaker family can be found in Rev. Muhlenberg's journal. His entry for Sunday, 29 May 1763, notes: "I went to the school house [in Philadelphia] where there was a widow with six children and two godparents or sponsors for each of them. Her husband had been of the Quaker persuasion and would not permit the children to be baptized while he was living. But since he had died, the mother and her friends desired that the children should become members of the Body of Christ through baptism. We spoke a little with the children according to their capacity, humbled ourselves before God in prayer and I baptized them according to the formula."[30] A search of the registers for St. Michael's and Zion Lutheran Church in Philadelphia shows that on this same date—29 May 1763—Muhlenberg baptized six children of Jacob Penninger, deceased, all born between 1752 and 1761; the mother's name was not given.[31]

Recognition of the movement into the Society of Friends is as important as the movement out. The Brosius family provides an interesting example. The lists of German immigrants for Philadelphia show four men with that surname as having arrived in the city between 1740 and 1748, and baptisms for several children with that family surname can be found in the registers of St. Michael's and Zion Lutheran Church in Philadelphia. Information on at least one branch of this German family can also be found in the Fallowfield Monthly Meeting records in Chester County, Pennsylvania. Those records list five sons of Henry and Mary Brosius born between 1794 and 1800.[32] Given the Quaker policy of recording information for members only, Henry Brosius, a descendant of German immigrants, sometime in the late-eighteenth century in Chester County must have become a Quaker.

Family historians will not find infants of questionable birth in Friends records. "Yielding to temptation" was sufficient reason for disownment. Elias Evans was disowned from the Philadelphia Monthly Meeting on 29 1st month 1768 for being guilty of unchastity and fathering an illegitimate child.[33] Katherine Whelin who "gave way to temptation" was found guilty of the sin of fornication and was disowned from the Uwchlan Monthly Meeting on 6th 7th month 1763.[34] Of interest, records of illegitimate births for Friends can sometimes be found in non-Quaker registers. A 1755 birth record for Maria Margaretha Priest, for example, is recorded in the registers of St. Michael's and Zion Lutheran Church in Philadelphia and the entry notes that the infant was the daughter of "John Priest a Quaker" and Elizabeth Strumm.[35]

Each of these examples convincingly demonstrates the need for genealogists working on Pennsylvania's early Quaker families to be cognizant of the movements of people between denominations. A family historian tracking down the Brosius family, for example, will spend a lot of time in blind alleys if the assumption is made that information on this family can be found in Quaker records only. Likewise, the descendants of Jacob Penninger, Daniel Creutz, and John Priest would have problems if they limited their search to Lutheran and Presbyterian records, and family historians working on Townsends would miss information on a branch of that family if Catholic church registers were ignored.

The limited vision or the "blind alley frustration" often experienced by family historians evokes a second cautionary watchword, again applicable to all genealogical research: Persistence. Blind alleys should always signal the need to explore different alleys; most destinations can be reached by a variety of routes.

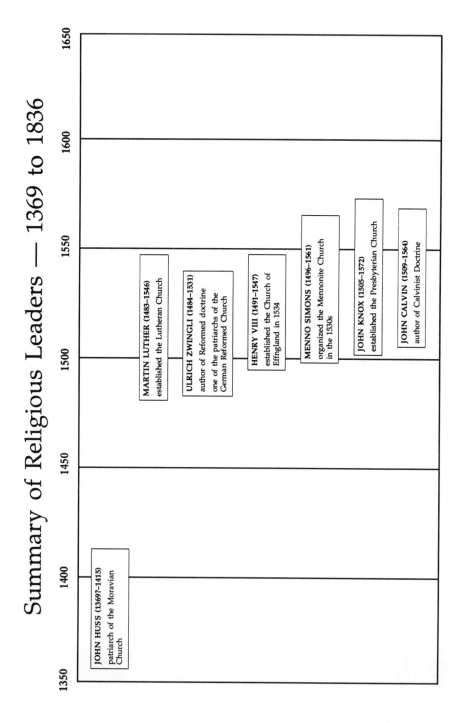

Summary of Religious Leaders — 1369 to 1836

JOHN HUSS (1369?–1415)
patriarch of the Moravian
Church

MARTIN LUTHER (1483–1546)
established the Lutheran Church

ULRICH ZWINGLI (1484–1531)
author of Reformed doctrine
one of the patriarchs of the
German Reformed Church

HENRY VIII (1491–1547)
established the Church of
Efmngland in 1534

MENNO SIMONS (1496–1561)
organized the Mennonite Church
in the 1530s

JOHN KNOX (1505–1572)
established the Presbyterian Church

JOHN CALVIN (1509–1564)
author of Calvinist Doctrine

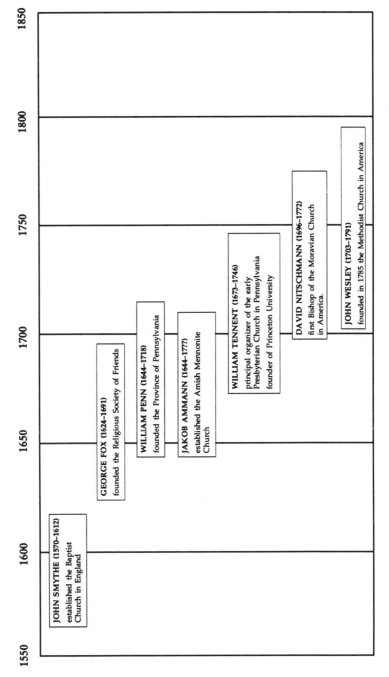

(continued on next page)

(note adjustment of dates in headings)

JOHN SMYTHE (1570–1612)
established the Baptist
Church in England

GEORGE FOX (1624–1691)
founded the Religious Society of Friends

WILLIAM PENN (1644–1718)
founded the Province of Pennsylvania

JAKOB AMMANN (1644–1727)
established the Amish Mennonite
Church

WILLIAM TENNENT (1673–1746)
principal organizer of the early
Presbyterian Church in Pennsylvania
founder of Princeton University

DAVID NITSCHMANN (1696–1772)
first Bishop of the Moravian Church
in America.

JOHN WESLEY (1703–1791)
founded in 1785 the Methodist Church in America

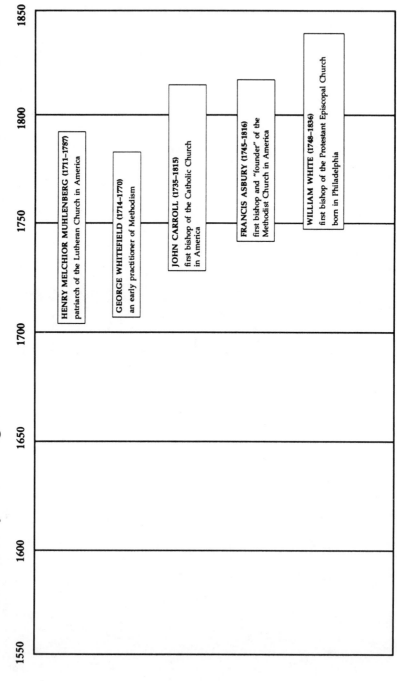

Summary of Religious Leaders — 1369 to 1836 (continued)

HENRY MELCHIOR MUHLENBERG (1711–1787)
patriarch of the Lutheran Church in America

GEORGE WHITEFIELD (1714–1770)
an early practitioner of Methodism

JOHN CARROLL (1735–1815)
first bishop of the Catholic Church in America

FRANCIS ASBURY (1745–1816)
first bishop and "founder" of the Methodist Church in America

WILLIAM WHITE (1748–1836)
first bishop of the Protestant Episcopal Church born in Philadelphia

Chapter 8

Evaluating the Evidence

More denominations were practicing a variety of religious beliefs in eighteenth-century Pennsylvania than in the rest of Christendom, and the range of beliefs concerning baptism were considerable. On one hand the Catholics, Lutherans, and Episcopalians argued that baptism was necessary for salvation and that parents should have their children baptized as soon as possible. On the other hand the Anabaptists and Baptists contended that infant baptism was meaningless. Mixed into this cauldron of ideas were the beliefs of George Fox, a Quaker, who contended that baptism was unnecessary for either infants or adults.

Readers may ask what relevance this discussion on the theology of baptism could possibly have to do with genealogical research. The answer is fairly simple. Families in eighteenth-century Pennsylvania lived in a unique situation. If they were immigrants from England or Germany, then they had been born into a structured environment wherein people did predictable things. Lutherans had their children baptized in Lutheran churches and members of the Church of England had their children baptized by an Anglican minister. When they arrived in Pennsylvania their situation changed. Everything was looser and more fluid. The societal structures they had relied upon in the past were no longer in place.

The choices available to Pennsylvania's immigrants seeking infant baptism in the 1710s and 1720s were limited because the Quakers, Mennonites, and Baptists maintained the majority of meeting houses and churches in the early years of the eighteenth century. The only denominations practicing infant baptism at the time were the Presbyterian, Swedish Lutheran, and Anglican churches. Immigrant families arriving in Philadelphia in those decades could choose to have their children baptized at one of these churches—or not at all.

In 1746, the Reformed minister Rev. Michael Schlatter described Pennsylvania as follows: ". . . Pennsylvania . . . is nothing less than a forest of large and heavy trees with some undergrowth. The people live far apart from each other and there are rarely more than 10 or 12 families to be found in a district of one hour in circumference."[1] More than one minister lamented the fact that he had to spend time constantly riding about "to far distant members and congregations."[2] Rev. Philip Boehm, in a letter citing the need for a Reformed minister in the Goshenhoppen area of Montgomery County, noted that some early settlers in the region traveled distances of up to twenty-five and thirty miles to bring children to his church for baptism. For the weak or the old or the pregnant, the trip was impossible. As a result, many children were not baptized until they were several years old.[3]

A survey of the number of ministers serving a single denomination affords an appreciation of the difficulties encountered by parents seeking baptism for their children. In 1753 sixteen ordained and eight unordained Lutheran ministers served an area extending from the Delaware River in the east to the border with Maryland in Adams County to the west.[4] This area included the present twelve counties of Philadelphia, Bucks, Northampton, Lehigh, Monroe, Montgomery, Berks, Chester, Lancaster, Lebanon, York, Dauphin, and Adams. On average, two Lutheran ministers were responsible for one county. This is a deceptive allocation, however, because these ministers were not evenly distributed; more Lutheran ministers served congregations in and around the towns and cities of Philadelphia and Lancaster than in other locations, leaving much of the rural areas totally unattended.

Lutheran immigrants at the time could have their children baptized at the local Lutheran church, but only if they were fortunate enough to settle in a location where Swedes or Germans had already organized a congregation, and only if that congregation happened to have an assigned minister. Most of our Lutheran ancestors were less fortunate. Many German immigrants, in order to pay their passage, were indentured as servants to Quakers and Presbyterians; consequently, they found themselves in those parts of Chester or Bucks counties, where there were no Lutheran churches.

In his journal, Rev. Henry Muhlenberg recorded the tale of one young family inconvenienced by indenture. Philip Jacob and Maria Magdalena Reichenbacher lived in an area of Bucks County that had been settled by Holland Dutch and Scotch-Irish families. These German indentured servants wanted to have their ten-months-old son Johannes baptized. They walked ten miles to Neshaminy because they had heard that Rev. Muhlenberg was scheduled to preach in the Dutch Reformed Church there, ". . . but since [Muhlenberg] had not come they had asked the Dutch Reformed preacher to baptize their child. . . ." The minister said he would do it with the understanding that the parents would promise to raise the child in the Dutch Reformed faith. Since the German Lutheran couple could not make that promise, Johannes was not baptized at that time and the parents returned home. Later they heard that Rev. Muhlenberg was at the home of John Christoph Rose, who operated a ferry crossing the Delaware River. On Friday, 20 July 1753, "they had come 5 miles to the Rose home to no avail because Muhlenberg had arrived too late." On the following day, Rev. Muhlenberg, in the company of John Christoph Rose, "journeyed to the [Reichenbacher] house and found the parents home. Since they were embarassed for lack of a sponsor Mr. Rose stepped in and [Muhlenberg] baptized the child. . . ."[5]

Evidence in Pennsylvania's eighteenth-century church records verifies that many parents encountered problems similar to that of Philip Jacob and Maria Magdalena Reichenbacher. Their search for a pastor of their own faith to baptize their children was not always succcessful. In the course of looking for an Anglican minister or Reformed pastor, they may have encoutered a Jesuit priest or Moravian missionary who they asked to perform the baptism. If any record was kept, the pertinent information was entered into a register of a faith different from that of the child's parents.

Thus, genealogists working on early Pennsylvania families must accept the fact that some family information may appear in the registers of more than one faith. In their search for alternative sources, researchers must know which churches were open to baptizing the infants of non-members and which were not—a knowledge that can come only from a broad understanding of baptismal practices and beliefs. The religious doctrine unique to each denomination determined the "rules of baptism."

In a continuum of religious thought (see chart on the following page), the Catholic Church holds the orthodox or base position with regard to baptismal practice. Given their total rejection of the sacrament by the Religious Society of Friends, Quakers hold the position on the opposite end. Between these two extremes are the remaining church denominations: the Lutherans and Episcopalians, the churches of the Reformed doctrine, and those churches adhering to Anabaptist and Baptist beliefs. The openness of denominations to baptizing infants of outsiders more or less mirrors this gradation in the theology of baptism. The denominations most willing to baptize infants of non-members were the Catholics, the Lutherans, and the Episcopalians. These three churches viewed baptism as salvation from sin and, interestingly, these same three churches practiced emergency or lay baptism.

The presence of Germanic surnames in eighteenth-century Anglican church registers indicates that, at least in the Philadelphia area, ministers of the Church of England were willing to baptize infants of non-members. A good example can be found in the records for Trinity Episcopal Church in Oxford Township, Philadelphia, where pastors recorded the baptisms of several children specifically identified as either "Palatine" or "German."[6] Researchers must be cautious, however, when searching Anglican baptismal records for German family names because many German surnames may not be easily recognizable in their Anglicized form.

The openness found in Anglican records can also be found in Lutheran registers. A large number of baptisms for Philadelphia's English families were performed by Lutheran pastors. Rev. Muhlenberg's journals frequently mention baptisms of English children. One notation, dated 19 November 1762, tells of his having been summoned by poor English families "where I had to baptize 2 sick children."[7]

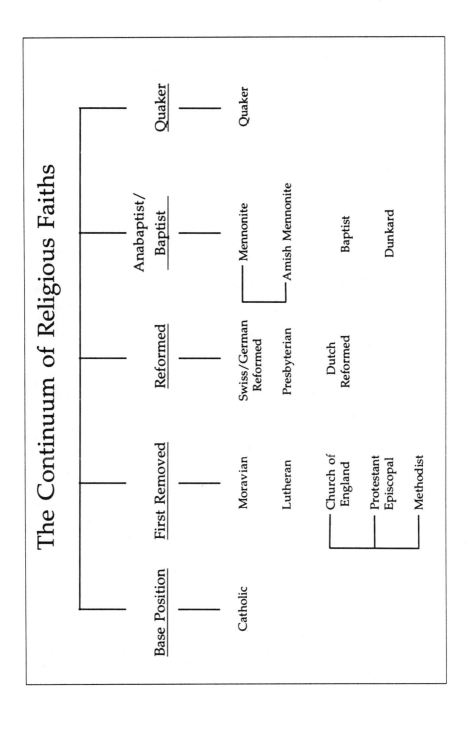

The Continuum of Religious Faiths

Base Position	First Removed	Reformed	Anabaptist/ Baptist	Quaker
Catholic	Moravian	Swiss/German Reformed	Mennonite	Quaker
	Lutheran	Presbyterian	Amish Mennonite	
	Church of England	Dutch Reformed	Baptist	
	Protestant Episcopal		Dunkard	
	Methodist			

Similarly, an entry in the records of St. Michael's and Zion include the baptism of William, son of Edward Pitts and Sara, baptized 1 March 1762. The pastor entering this record noted that the parents were "both English."[8]

Lutheran clergy extended their willingness to baptize children of non-members to include different ethnic heritage as well as different faith. The entry below, found in the St. Michael's and Zion register, translates in part as follows: "Andreas Götz and his wife, Maria Elisabeth, Catholics living in Kensington."

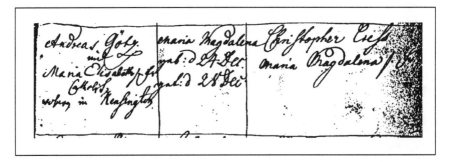

Another entry appearing in the same register lists Joseph Hillburn, born 4 May 1769, baptized 21 July 1769, son of Thomas Hillburn, "a Quaker,"and the mother the "daughter of Benjamin Johnson of Swedish extraction."[9] The child of an Anabaptist shows up in the 1759 records of the Swedish Lutheran Church in Philadelphia: George, son of Thomas and Hannah Domon, born 2 July 1759. The entry notes, "The father was anabaptist [possibly Mennonite] but the mother was protestant and was excedingly anxious that the child should be baptized."[10] Of interest, the minister further noted that this baptism was performed privately.

English parents living in Philadelphia during the Revolutionary War found the Lutheran clergy's willingness to baptize infants of non-members quite useful. The occupation of that city by British troops from 26 September 1777 until 18 June 1778 caused considerable disruption in normal church activities, and the Anglican congregations were particularly stressed. The records of a Lutheran minister, Rev. John Christopher Kunze, one of the few clergy who remained in the beleaguered city, lists at least 193 children who were baptized during

the period of British occupation. The surnames for many of those infants indicates quite clearly that they were children of English parents.[11]

An openness in the Catholic Church to baptizing non-members
is similar to that of the Lutherans, illustrated by the fact that records
can be found wherein Catholic priests did not hesitate to baptize
the infants of protestant parents. The records of St. Joseph's Catholic
Church in Philadelphia, for example, include many baptismal entries
for which parents are noted as "protestant."

Baptisms of African-American slaves and "free Negroes" were also
recorded in the registers of the Swedish Lutheran Church, the German
Lutheran Church, the Catholic Church, and the Anglican Church. The
baptismal entry for a Negro manservant of the "y^e Gov." can be found
in the 1717 Christ Church (Philadelphia) register illustrated below:

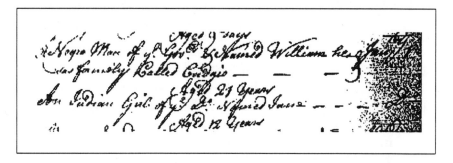

Note that a twelve-year-old Indian girl of "y^e D^o" ("the ditto"—the
governor) was also baptized the same day.

Next in the continuum of religious thought in eighteenth-century
Pennsylvania denominations are the churches of the Reformed doctrine: the Presbyterian, Reformed, and Dutch Reformed. Baptism according to Reformed theology is a sign or seal of salvation through
Christ's sacrifice. Children who die unbaptized are saved, and this im-
plied salvation for unbaptized infants mitigates the urgency to perform the rite. The denominations following the Reformed tradition
dropped emergency baptism from their practice. Surviving session records and other documents suggest that both the Presbyterian and Reformed churches raised barriers to the rite—actions that limited
access by outsiders. This kind of impediment was experienced by

Philip Jacob Reichenbacher (mentioned earlier in this chapter) when the Dutch Reformed minister agreed to baptize his son Johannes only on the condition that the infant would be raised in the Dutch Reformed Church.

Any researcher who might consider using Germanic surnames and African-American baptisms as a gauge of openness will find clear evidence that the Presbyterian Church was not open to baptizing the infants of non-members. A search for Germanic surnames and African-American baptisms in more than five thousand Presbyterian baptismal records yielded only thirty. All of the seven African-American baptisms took place in Philadelphia churches and all were recorded in the 1770s; all twenty-three German baptisms appear in the records of the Abington Presbyterian Church, Montgomery County.

Information about one of the African-American baptisms found in the records of Scots Presbyterian Church, Philadelphia, suggests that many—if not all—of these baptisms were probably performed for children of church members. When the pastor of the Scots Presbyterian Church, Rev. William Marshall, recorded the baptism of Issac Worley Till, son of Hannah, a free Negro woman, he noted that she was "in full communion with the church."[12] Clearly, this is an entry for the son of a Negro member of a Presbyterian Church. This one confirmed baptism sends a clear signal that the other six African-American baptisms, all found in the Second Presbyterian Church register, were probably also performed for members of that church.

The baptismal records for the twenty-three German children covered infants from three families: Vetter/Fetters, Ottinger, and Vetzer. All four of William Ottinger's children were baptized on the same day, 4 January 1777, and three of Frederick Vetzer's children were baptized 11 April 1774.[13] The entry for the fourth child of Frederick Vetzer confirms an earlier baptism: "the eldest daughter Elizabeth having been many years before baptized by the Rev. Mr. Milleberry."[14] Baptisms of fifteen children in the Vetter/Fetters family extends over a considerable period of time—from 1765 to 1799. This long-term affliation of the Vetter/Fetters family suggests that they were church members.

In terms of openness, the Reformed Church found itself somewhere between the Presbyterians, who restricted baptism, and the Lutheran and Anglican churches, where baptism was open to anyone.

The 1755 resolution of the German Reformed Coetus, stating that "Holy Baptism shall not be administered to a stranger except in case of necessity," would seem to indicate that at least some restrictions were placed on the adminstration of the rite to non-members.[15]

Research on German families in Pennsylvania reveals that many Reformed pastors baptized the infants of Lutheran parents, but in the absence of detailed studies on these families, it is difficult to claim that Reformed ministers were open to baptizing infants of non-members. Baptismal discipline in the Reformed Church required that only one parent be a communicant member, so it is quite possible that many of the so-called "Lutheran baptisms" appear only because one of the parents was a confirmed member in the Reformed Church. The possibility also exists that, given the union arrangements between many Lutheran and Reformed congregations in rural Pennsylvania where these churches shared the same building, Reformed ministers took a relaxed attitude toward baptizing the infants of Lutheran parents. In addition to the fact that a significant number of these early congregations were frequently without the services of a pastor, many Reformed pastors may have invoked the rule as adopted by the Coetus allowing them to perform baptisms for strangers "in case of necessity" when a Lutheran minister was not available to baptize children of Lutheran church members.

Genealogists searching Lutheran records will find that several ministers recorded in their church registers the denomination of the parents seeking baptism. This meticulous record-keeping, of course, makes it easier to identify non-member baptisms. Reformed Church registers, in most cases, do not furnish comparable information. An exception can be found in one record of the Reformed Church, Philadelphia, where a Reformed minister entered similar data. That record, however, is incomplete.

In the absence of definitive data designating a specific denomination, the only method of gauging the willingness of Reformed mininsters to baptize infants of non-members is to search for non- Germanic surnames and non-ethnic baptisms. English and African-American baptisms in Reformed registers are not plentiful. Only one African-American baptism and only seven English surnames for registered baptisms appear prior to 1780 in the records of the two Philadelphia

Reformed churches. The two Lutheran church registers for Philadelphia list twelve pre-1780 African-American baptisms.

Churches practicing Anabaptist and Baptist doctrine occupy the next position on the continuum, but given their beliefs on infant baptism it is unlikely that any parent would have approached a Mennonite, Baptist or Dunkard/Brethern minister to have a child baptized.

Holding the final position in the continuum are the Quakers. As previously noted, the Religious Society of Friends never practiced the sacramental rite of baptism, hence Friend's meeting records have little relevance in terms of the issues of openness and baptism.

Any advantages that can be gained from knowing about baptismal practices and beliefs is not limited to finding alternative source records for family information. That knowledge can also afford a far greater insight into the records that the genealogist has already searched. The baptismal record of Elizabeth Flemming recorded in the register of St. Michael's and Zion Lutheran Church, Philadelphia, provides an interesting example. Elizabeth was the daughter of John and Margaretha Flemming. In recording this baptism, the Lutheran pastor noted that "the Scotchman and his wife, the parents, were the sponsors."[16] While the mother of the child may have been German, the "Scotchman" was undoubtedly Presbyterian. As discussed in this text, the traditions of his faith would dictate that he was responsible for the spiritual welfare of his child. Even though this baptism was performed by a Lutheran pastor, John Flemming and his wife accepted the role of sponsors and pledged the vows on behalf of their daughter.

For another example wherein a genealogist's knowledge of baptismal practice gives greater meaning to the furnished information, consider this baptismal entry for Margaret Johnstone in the Tinicum Presbyterian Church register: "Abraham Johnstone and his wife acknowledged their sorrow on being guilty of fornication and had their child baptized by name Margaret July 22 1770."[17] The earlier discussion about Presbyterian beliefs and practices noted the role the session played in affording members access to the sacraments. It is interesting to note that this baptismal entry does not record the birth as illegitimate, leading to the conclusion that Abraham Johnstone and his unnamed wife obviously went before the session to acknowledge their sorrow. Equally important, they were married sometime between Margaret's conception and birth. Their "sin" came about because Margaret was born less than nine months after that marriage. For anyone working on the Johnstone family, this record obviously provides information on the baptism of Margaret and the names of her parents. But for the genealogist who knows and understands the baptismal practices of the Presbyterian Church, this record provides even more information—it also establishes the approximate marriage date of Margaret's parents.

A knowledge of baptismal practices can promote a greater depth of understanding in other ways. Family historians conditioned to finding records wherein family members or friends of the same socio-economic status are named as baptismal sponsors would probably find the following entry for an early Pennsylvania settler rather disturbing, and maybe even question its authenticity: Stephen Steiger, was born on 14 August 1688 in Bohemia. Stephen's father, Nicholas Steiger, is identified as a wagon master in the army. Named as sponsors for the infant are "the most illustrious Stephen Stanville, Gentleman and his wife Elizabeth Rogerina." Witness to the event is the Jesuit priest, Johannes Schoborning Stanville.[18] Clearly the Gentleman Stephen Stanville and his wife had superior social rank to the "wagon master," Nicholas Steiger. Knowing the background of baptismal practices of the church in the medieval period helps explain this record. As detailed earlier, it was customary during this period to have someone of superior social rank as a sponsor at a baptism. The Steiger record shows that this tradition among Catholics in central Europe persisted well into the seventeenth century.

Adherents to the Catholic faith in Pennsylvania practiced the centuries-old tradition of emergency baptism, and numerous entries can be found in Catholic registers for infants who were "baptized privately." Sponsors for these baptisms are frequently not named. A congizance of early Catholic procedures will alert genealogists to the fact that these entries are probably for infants baptized by one of the parents, the midwife, or the priest.

Presbyterian parents wanting baptism for their children had to be members in good standing, meaning that both parents had to be baptized members of the church. Many of the adult baptisms found in Presbyterian church registers are more fully explained by understanding Presbyterian Church practices and procedures, i.e., both parents had to be baptized before a child or infant could be baptized in the Presbyterian Church. Thus, consider the following example: Joseph Cornelius was baptized on 17 May 1772 by the minister of the Second Presbyterian Church in Philadelphia, whose pastor noted in the record that this person was baptized as an adult. Roughly two months later, on 18 July 1772, two children of Joseph Cornelius and his wife were baptized: William, born 4 April 1768, and Elizabeth, born 23 August 1770.[19] Interestingly, both children were born before their father's baptism, but their baptisms, rather than taking place at the same time, were performed at a later date. Furthermore, it can be assumed that Joseph's wife was already a baptized member of the Presbyterian Church prior to 1772. This entry is typical for many that can be found in Pennsylvania's early church registers—that is, one or both parents were baptized at roughly the same time as one or more of their children, but not necessarily on the same date.

Many adults living in Pennsylvania in the eighteenth century were unbaptized primarily for two reasons: Parents often could not find ministers to baptize infants, so their children grew up unbaptized, or children were born into a faith that held to the belief that infant baptism had no meaning. As the numbers of congregations and churches grew and the availability of ministers increased, many of these unbaptized adults sought church membership and/or wanted to have their own children baptized.

As explained earlier in this text, with the exception of the Religious Society of Friends, each of the major religious denominations in Pennsylvania retained the traditional belief that baptism constituted entrance into the church. At times, the adult also confirmed a devotion to the principles followed by a particular church. A primary illustration of this point can be found in an entry in the register of the First Reformed Church in Philadelphia for Anna Maria Keim, baptized as an adult on 18 September 1761. The pastor who entered Anna Maria's baptism in the register added the comment, "and thereafter openly confirmed in the church with others."[20] Similar entries for young adults who were baptized just prior to confirmation can be found in other Reformed and Lutheran church registers.

It is important to remember that eighteenth-century baptismal records are always potentially more useful to the family historian who understands the variety of and differences between prevalent religious practice of the day. The right to become a communicant member of many of these churches generated from baptism rather than from confirmation. Knowledge of the relationship between confirmation and baptism can be useful to the genealogist in other ways. Within religious denominations where infant baptism was practiced, ministers would not confirm an unbaptized candidate for church membership without prior baptism. Admittedly, confirmation records do not provide the detailed information the genealogist seeks in a baptismal record. But given the difficulties of finding baptismal records for many people in Pennsylvania in the eighteenth century, confirmation records are at least proof that the baptism did, in fact, take place.

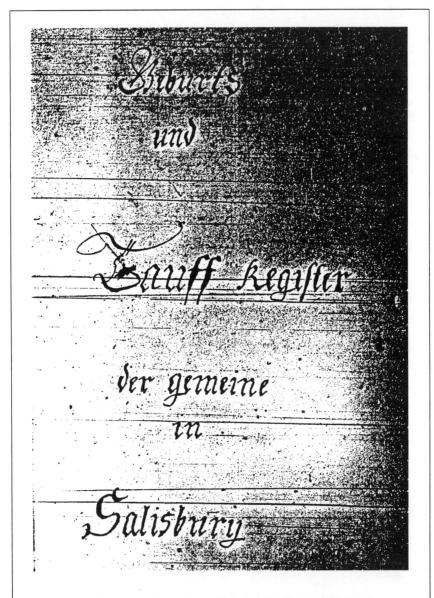

Title page to an early birth and baptismal register of Salisbury
Moravian Church, Salisbury Township (now Emmaus), Lehigh County.

Chapter 9

About Baptismal Registers

Many problems that genealogists find in working with Pennsyl-vania's early baptismal registers are directly related to unset-tled conditions in the colonial province. The major considerations for all early immigrants who came to William Penn's colony were the es-sentials of life: food, clothing, and shelter. And to acquire any of these articles, the colonists first had to clear the land of trees and under-brush. Only after basic needs were met could settlers proceed with the business of founding churches and meeting houses. The baptismal register, the principal concern of the genealogist, came even later— that is, a church record could be opened only after a minister was in place and a book had been acquired. But evidence will show these ac-tivities rarely took place concurrently or in a uniform manner.

The actual process of establishing churches was similar for most re-ligious groups. After a sufficient number of people had settled in any given area, they could band together to form a congregation. This small group gathered, probably in someone's house, barn, or field, where a worship service was held. If the group could manage to grow and meet on a regular basis, then some thought was given to securing property and building a school, meeting house, or perhaps a church. Then these early congregations had to secure the services of a minis-ter. Early on, most congregations were forced to rely on the services of schoolmasters and so-called "itinerant" preachers whose qualifications were questionable at best. Later, when a more qualified pastor finally answered his call to service, evidence indicates that many congregations and meetings had difficulty securing a record book. The result was that many early baptisms were not recorded.

The Anglican Church was one of the earliest to organize in Philadelphia. A clause in William Penn's charter afforded members of the Church of England an opportunity to establish a church in the Quaker colony. According to the terms of the charter, members of the Anglican Church could request a cleric if a group of twenty or more could be assembled. In 1695 the required number met, appointed a vestry, and purchased a lot at Second and High streets. Having fulfilled Penn's requirements, the congregation sent a request for a minister to the Bishop of London. Three years later, the first Anglican pastor of Christ Church arrived in Philadelphia to serve the small but growing congregation.[1]

The procedure for establishing Reformed and Lutheran congregations was somewhat similar to the one used by the Anglicans in 1695. Conrad Tempelman, an early Reformed minister in Lancaster, described the process in a 1733 letter he sent to Holland:

> The church at Chanastocka had its origins in the year 1725, with a small gathering in houses here and there, with the reading of a sermon and with song and prayer . . . but on account of the lack of a minister, without the administration of baptism and the Lord's Supper.[2]

Tempelman's description is similar to Muhlenberg's portrayal of how Reed's Church in Berks County organized:

> . . . a number of Lutherans among them [Conrad] Weiser, many years ago bought a piece of land and built a wooden church on it and also erected a schoolhouse. They used to have a sermon read in the church on Sundays and occasionally they permitted an itinerant preacher to preach there until finally there arrived a man named [Casper] Leitbecker. At first this man took over reading but eventually he began to act as a preacher . . . .[3]

Securing property or land for the church or schoolhouse and graveyard was an important step in the process. It meant a group was meeting on a regular basis; together they could pool enough money either to apply for a warrant or, perhaps, to purchase a small tract from one of the members. The resultant warrant or deed is often the first evidence that a congregation existed or was in the process of forming. Most deeds or patents contain some reference to the tract being used "for a burying ground and school house." Sometimes the deed specified "for the use of the united Lutheran and Reformed Congregation."[4]

The initial stages of establishing a Presbyterian Church were similar to the process used by Lutheran and Reformed congregations. A few settlers in an area came together to form a society; once that society was established, the new congregation went about the business of acquiring a piece of land and building a meeting house.[5]

The easiest part was joining together to start the church and purchase land. The more difficult task was securing a pastor—the person who ultimately had the responsibilities of performing the baptism and recording that baptism in the church register. Denominations depending on ordained pastors faced two problems: first, they had to find a qualified person willing to serve their congregation; then they had to keep him. The availability of ministers was not as serious a problem for Quakers and Mennonites as for other denominations because these two secured ministers from within their own group.

Initially many of the early Lutheran and Reformed congregations had to settle for unordained itinerants who went from place to place and had neither a fixed home nor a permanent congregation. On Sundays they read a sermon or, if inspired, preached. As Muhlenberg notes, they were paid to baptize children and give communion. This was the way that they made their living; their credentials were questionable at best. One Lutheran itinerant, Peter Mischler, was examined by the Lutheran Ministerium in 1769, and it was concluded that he "cannot write a single letter of the alphabet properly, that he cannot spell, and that he cannot compose anything with connected thoughts or acceptable style."[6] Obviously, keeping a baptismal register or church book was beyond Peter Mischler's capabilities.

Other so-called ministers were schoolmasters who also began to preach. They performed an invaluable service in the absence of regular pastors, filling a void and providing solace and comfort to many recent immigrants in need of spiritual help or, perhaps, baptism for a dying infant or child. Several of these schoolmasters eventually received ordination, but most were not schooled in the rigorous traditions of professional Lutheran and Reformed pastors—that is, they were not conditioned to keeping records of their pastoral acts.

Other itinerants known to baptize infants in Pennsylvania and elsewhere were the Moravian Brethren who worked out of Bethlehem. The diaries of their travels throughout Pennsylvania, Maryland, western Virginia, and North Carolina provide detailed accounts of encounters with early settlers seeking baptism for their children. On 14 February 1749, the Moravian missionary Sven Roseen had traveled through the Delaware Water Gap to the home of Joh. Andreas Neu, who had immigrated to Pennsylvania from near Fraensheim in Germany. Neu had settled on the banks of the Delaware River in an area where there were no organized churches. While at the Neu home, Roseen was approached by Neu's neighbor who asked

> . . . whether I were the minister, and whether I would not baptize his two children. I went with him into his house, and as I came in the children were very friendly toward me. I considered the request, thought of the texts of the day and the words of the Saviour, (II Cor. 9: 15 and Acts 20: 35) and how the heavenly Father had brought it about that I should meet the father of the children, and so had the neighbors of Neu called, Thomas Quick and Richard Howel. Both the Howels had been good friends of Shaw [Brother Joseph Shaw] in Walpack, and were now living on the other side of the Delaware, where Paulins Creek empties into the river. When they heard that a brother from Bethlehem was present they brought their daughter, and promised to rear the child for the Saviour. She could not say anything but her expression did speak, and I found nothing to hinder the child's baptism. I baptized the three infants into the death of Jesus, with earnest petition to the Father, the Son and the Holy Ghost after I had said all to the parents that I deemed necessary.[7]

Again, securing a minister was the more difficult part of the process for Presbyterian churches as well. A local layman or school teacher was usually the first to preach and conduct services. He was followed by an ordained minister who came into the area only occasionally. As the congregation became more firmly established, the number of visits by the ordained minister increased and followed a more regular schedule—perhaps once a month. When the contributing membership was sufficient to support the cost of a minister, a call was placed to a regular pastor. Depending on the area and the size of the congregations, a minister might supply several churches.[8]

The growth of the Presbyterian Church in Pennsylvania in the middle decades of the eighteenth century was fairly rapid, and this growth did not go unnoticed by Muhlenberg. On 4 February 1765, he wrote in his journal,

> The English Presbyterian Church is growing so rapidly among the English in America that in a few years it will surpass the Episcopal and all the rest of us. . . . [Growth in Presbyterian membership] is due to the fact that they have established seminaries in various places and educate their own ministers, keep strict discipline and tolerate no ministers except those who have good moral character. . . .[9]

Here Rev. Muhlenberg touched on a topic that affected the growth rate of all denominations—the settlers' inability to attract qualified ministers to supply the ever-increasing number of congregations. The Coetus of the Reformed Church, for example, could not ordain ministers in Pennsylvania; thus, Reformed congregations were dependent upon the supply of ministers from Europe. Ministers in the Anglican Church pursued their education and and received ordination in England— meaning that candidates for the ministry in the Anglican Church born in the American Colonies had to return to the mother country. The situation for the Lutheran Church was easier only to the extent that the German fathers in Halle placed no limitations on the ability of the Ministerium to ordain qualified candidates for the ministry; in Pennsylvania, however, the pool of potential candidates was never great. As for the Presbyterians, they had established a school in Bucks County (see Muhlenberg's reference above) where candidates for the ministry were provided with appropriate education, but even that did not solve the problem. At some time or another, fully one-half of the Presbyterian churches in Pennsylvania functioned without the services of a minister.[10]

Minister vacancies were a serious problem for each of these denominations. Early in the eighteenth century, the Swedish Lutheran Church in Philadelphia was without a pastor for ten years; from 1722 until 1726, Christ Church in Philadelphia had no rector. In 1742 Anglican cleric Rev. Richard Backhouse noted that "this providence is now becoming exceedingly populous and there are many large congregations of Church people [Anglicans] who being quite destitute of Church of England Ministers are to their great grief obliged to herd among the Presbyterians."[11] A letter, sent in 1760 to the Society for the Propagation of the Gospel in London, pleaded for an Anglican minister to serve the congregation in Berks County.[12] The letter went on to note that Roman Catholic priests in the area were making converts. In 1759 the minutes for the Presbytery of Donegal listed eight congregations under its jurisdiction without a pastor.[13] As late as 1783, twenty congregations in the Reformed church had no assigned minister.[14]

The inability of most churches to attract and keep ministers had serious repercussions on baptismal records. Fundamentally stated, the intermittent absence of ministers at many churches resulted in periodic intervals in baptismal registers when no baptisms were recorded. The family historian working with those registers must develop an awareness of these intervals wherein baptismal records simply do not exist.

An analysis of Pennsylvania's early church records frequently reveals a lapse of time between the date a congregation was organized and the dates that initial entries appear in the church register. This situation was not unique to any one church or denomination—delays can be found in virtually every early Pennsylvania church or meeting record. The evidence suggests that this gap or delay exists because a book was not available. As a result, genealogists will experience difficulty finding baptismal records for many of Pennsylvania's earliest families.

The first rector of Christ Church, Rev. Thomas Clayton, arrived in Philadelphia in 1698. Extant baptismal records for that congregation, however, begin eleven years later. Rev. Evan Evans, Rev. Clayton's successor, arrived in Philadelphia in 1700 and returned to England in 1707 for personal reasons. After returning to Philadelphia in 1709, Rev. Evans kept a register for Christ Church—its first—which began in the year of his return to the Colonies.

A second record book for Christ Church was begun in 1720, and on the inside cover of this book is the imprint (reproduced on the following page) of the London stationer where the book was purchased: "Thomas Ridge Stationer and Importer at the Boarshead in Cornhill near Stocks Market London." The imprint notes that the company was a supplier of ". . . paper or books with all sorts of large ledgers or journals of any size and thickness."[15] Since the second record book came to Philadelphia from London, one cannot help but wonder whether the first book may have been purchased there as well. If that was the case, then it may not be coincidental that the first record book for Christ Church begins in 1709 because Rev. Evans brought a record book to Pennsylvania from England wherein he could record the sacramental acts of his congregation. (Reproduction of a page from Rev. Evans' 1709 baptismal record book can be found on page 34.)

While visiting London in 1708, Rev. Evans reported to his superiors that his activites were not restricted to Philadelphia; he also officiated in Chester, Chichester, Maidenhead, Upland, Evesham in west Jersey, Montgomery, Radnor, and Oxford. Evans further notes that in these places "he had baptized 800 adults and children."[16] The fact that Rev. Evans was able to make such a detailed report in London suggests that he probably kept a personal record of his activities during his initial years in Philadelphia. If a permanent record of those 800 baptisms were ever made, however, it has either been lost, misplaced—or perhaps, was left in London.

Record-keeping irregularities were not unique to Christ Church. In fact, practically every eighteenth-century Pennsylvania congregation was plagued with similar problems. The Quakers—ordinarily known for their meticulous records—apparently experienced difficulty in securing permanent record books. The first business meeting of the Philadelphia Friends took place on 9 11th month 1682 and, among other things it was agreed ". . . that the necessary books be provided for. . . ."[17] The introduction to the Philadelphia Monthly Meeting record reads: "A Book Began by Robert Ewer the 1st of the 11th Month 1689 and to be continued till further order of the Monthly Meeting."[18] Simply put, there was a delay of seven years between the initial gathering of the Philadelphia Monthly Meeting in 1682, when the call was made to obtain a record book, and the date these records actually

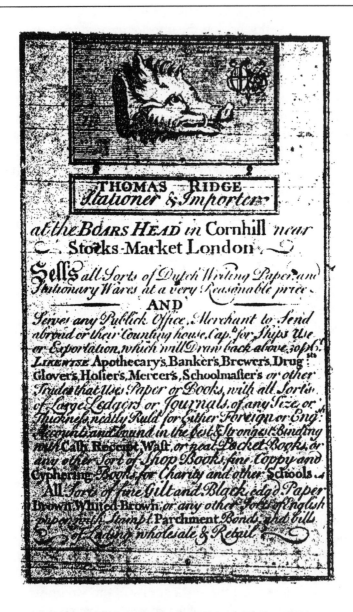

Imprint of London stationer and importer Thomas Ridge.

begin. The first birth recorded in this Monthly Meeting record is that of Joseph Wharton, son of Thomas and Rachel Wharton, born 25 9th month 1689.[19] All pre-1689 birth records in this book were "back filled," either from some previous record or from memory.

A similar time delay can also be found in other Monthly Meeting registers. Abington Monthly Meeting in Montgomery County was established in 1682, and the need to acquire a record book was noted at the Monthly Meeting held on the 3rd day of the 7th month 1683.[20] Apparently a permanent record was not secured for another thirty-five years, because the inside title page for that meeting record reads: "Abington Monthly Meeting Book Containing a Chronologie of the most Material Occurrences and Transactions that have been acted and done, in the said Meeting & c. Since ye first Settlement thereof. Transcribed From Sundry Manuscripts By George Boone 1718."[21]

Here the evidence leaves no doubt that the permanent record was copied from earlier maunscripts. (The title page from the 1718 Abbington Monthly Meeting Book is reproduced on the following page.)

One of the earliest business meetings for the Chester Friends was held on the 11th day of the 7th Month 1682. At that meeting it was ordered ". . . that large books being fitt for the servis of the monthly and quarterly meetings be provided against the next monthly meeting. Robert Wade is desired to gett the said books."[22] Wade was more successful in securing a book than his Philadelphia counterpart in that a book for the Chester Monthly Meeting exists from 1682. This extant book, which may have come from England in 1682 with the initial immigration of Friends, is rather interesting. The records of the business affairs of the Chester Monthly Meeting from 1682 to 1707 were entered in the front of the book starting on the first page, and the vital records for the Meeting were entered on the very last page moving in reverse order toward the front of the book. A second record book was begun for the Chester Monthly Meeting in 1708, into which all of the earlier entries from the first book were recopied. (See page 107 for a reproduction of this book's cover.)

The history of Pennsylvania's Lutheran and Reformed churches shows that in the 1720s, 1730s, and early 1740s, settlers banded together to form congregations. Other than the personal register of

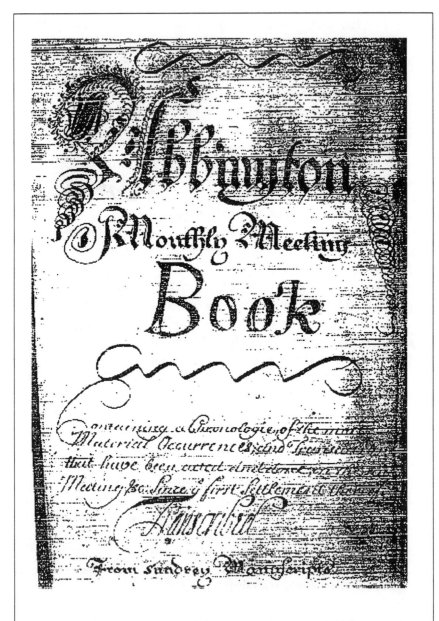

Title page from the 1718 Abbington Monthly Meeting Book.

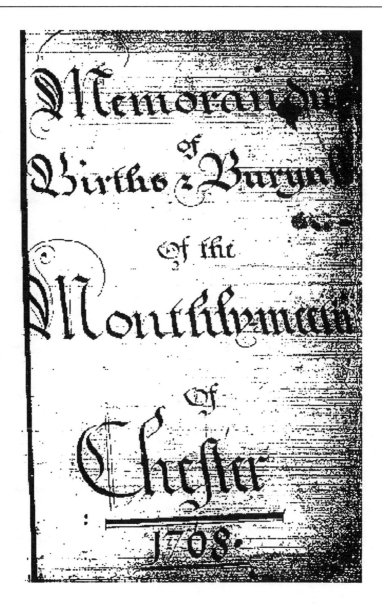

Cover of the 1708 Chester Monthly Meeting register.

Rev. John Casper Stoever (1707–1779) and some entries he made in church registers, however, little remains in the way of vital records from this time period. This void poses serious problems for genealogists working on Pennsylvania's German families.

The oldest German Lutheran Church in Pennsylvania is the New Hanover Lutheran Church in Montgomery County, founded in 1717 or 1718. (See page 26 for the reproduction of a page from one of this church's baptismal registers.) A succession of ministers served the congregation for the next twenty-four years, but not continuously. The extant baptismal register for this church begins in 1742 with the entries of Rev. Henry Muhlenberg; the only pre-1742 baptismal records that survive for this congregation are those Rev. Stoever recorded in his personal register.

The Reformed Congregation in New Hanover, called Falckner Swamp, was served by John Philip Boehm (1683–1749), a schoolmaster turned pastor. Boehm, who is given credit for starting the German Reformed Church in Pennsylvania, served this congregation from 1725 to 1748. His successor, Rev. Joh. Philipp Leydich (1715–1784), who served the church from 1748 until 1765, began the only known early baptismal register for this congregation. (A reproduction of the title page from Leydich's register appears on page 44.) Although Boehm undoubtedly baptized infants during his twenty-three years of service to the Falckner Swamp Church, any records he may have kept have not survived.

Six pastors ministered to the Lutheran Congregation in Philadelphia over a ten-year period in a rented building described by Count Zinzendorf as "a miserable shed" and by Muhlenberg as a "leaky slaughterhouse."[23] Muhlenberg, the seventh pastor to serve the congregation, initiated the building of a church in 1743 and started keeping a record book in 1745. Again, the only pre-1742 baptismal records that survive for this congregation are those recorded by Rev. Stoever in his own personal register.

The scarcity of early baptismal records is not unique to Lutheran and Reformed churches in Philadelphia and Montgomery counties; it is a general rule that can be applied to almost all of the early Lutheran and Reformed churches in southeastern Pennsylvania. The problem can probably be attributed to a number of things. Among them—and a primary factor—was the price and availability of a book. An October 1752 entry in the Minutes of the Coetus of the Reformed Church states that folio books ". . . bound in parchment, intended for baptisms and church records. . ." were purchased in Holland for the use of ministers and churches in Pennsylvania. These books were purchased by the President of the Coetus at a price of ". . .44 guilders 10 stuivers. . . ."[24] No record was left to indicate which of the eleven ministers present at the meeting took books for their congregations, but a record book was an unaffordable luxury for many of these small country congregations who, according to the same Minutes, could barely collect enough money to pay their pastor.

However difficult, the obstacles faced by genealogists working with Lutheran, Reformed, or Episcopalian baptismal records seem surmountable when compared with those faced by those working with Presbyterian registers. As previously noted, the Lutheran, Reformed, and Episcopalian churches achieved state recognition in their respective countries of origin. This "official" status enabled them to develop a tradition of baptismal record-keeping. The Presbyterian Church in England was not recognized as a legitimate church, and disincentives to maintaining records by non-conformist churches became part of the legal code of Great Britain in the late-seventeenth century. Thus, Presbyterian ministers working in Pennsylvania in the early-eighteenth to mid-eighteenth century did not employ a tradition of maintaining baptismal records as did their Lutheran, Reformed, and Episcopalian associates. As stated previously in this text, only three pre-1760 Presbyterian church registers exist for the twelve Presbyterian congregations in the southeastern Pennsylvania counties of Bucks, Montgomery, Philadelphia, Chester, Northampton, and Delaware. A closer examination of those extant registers actually reduces the number to one, because one of the two remaining records is a personal register and the other a compilation taken from prior lists.

Rev. Jedediah Andrews (1674–1747) was responsible for establishing the First Presbyterian Church in Philadelphia in 1698. His personal register of baptisms, started in the year he was ordained, includes a list of 1,746 children and adults baptized between 14 December 1701 and 7 October 1746.[25] Rev. Andrews' personal register is contained within the collections of the Presbyterian Historical Society in Philadelphia. A comparsion of that register with a microfilm of a record identified as "A Register of Baptisms for the Use of the First Presbyterian Church in the City of Philadelphia, 1701–1746," shows these two records are virtually identical.[26] The only conclusion that can be drawn is that the "Register of Baptisms" was never maintained for the First Presbyterian Church in Philadelphia as a church record per se; the record that has since become identified as the register of this Philadelphia church was initially kept as a personal register.

Efforts to maintain a church register for the First Presbyterian congregation commenced in 1763. At a meeting of church leaders held on 5 January 1763, it was decided that "[a]s it is of Importance that an exact Register be kept of the Marriages, Births, Baptisms & Burials of the congregation ordered That three books be provided one for Mr. Cross, one for Doct. Allison and one for Mr. Ewing in which they may enter all they marry and baptize. . . ."[27] In December 1763, Rev. Ewing turned over to the secretary of the church a list of baptisms and marriages that he had performed after he was hired as the minister of the congregation in 1760. That list of fifty-two baptisms and sixty-five marriages was incorporated into the church register.[28]

Baptismal records from 1746 through 1760 for the First Presbyterian Church have not been located, and many researchers have assumed that the records were lost. Given the preponderance of evidence that a church register was not maintained prior to 1763, an assumption that those records were lost is probably in error. If any pastoral acts from 1746 to 1760 were recorded, those records would have been in the form of a personal register kept by Rev. Robert Cross who served this congregation from 1739 until 1758. The decision by church elders to provide Rev. Cross with a book to record baptisms and marriages in 1763 suggests that he probably did not maintain a personal register before that date.

Historical information in the form of session and church records for the Second Presbyterian Church in Philadelphia provides interesting detail on how that particular register came to exist. Evidently a prior list was used to compile the church register. The Second Presbyterian Church was organized in 1743 by Gilbert Tennent (1701–1764) and a baptismal register starting in 1745 does exist for this congregation. The record from 1745 until 1761 is fairly consistent in that there are entries each year. A feature distinguishing this particular register from other similar records is the identification of the minister who baptized each child. A total of 154 baptisms were recorded between 1745 and 1761, and Rev. Gilbert Tennent is listed as the minister responsible for 136. Between 1761 and 1769 no baptisms were recorded because this church did not have a regular pastor; Rev. Tennent died in 1764 and his replacement, Rev. James Sproat (1743–1793), was not hired until October 1768.[29]

The following entry in the session record from the church, dated 11 January 1769, shows that the "official" church register was actually initiated in 1769:

> The session also taking into consideration the great impor-tance not only in religious but civil matters and have a regular record of all baptisms, marriages and burials in the congrega-tion and finding thro. our unsettled state and other circumstances that is has not hitherto been done do agree in the future the Rev. Sprout be rquested to keep the same and Messrs Rhea and Bayard are appointed to prepare a book for the said purpose and to collect such records as are to be found and cause them to be fairly transcribed into said book and then deliver it to Mr. Sprout with such original Records as they can obtain to be kept for the use of the church.[30]

The next set of entries in the church register begins on 28 February 1769, a little more than a month after the session ordered that a record book be kept.

The two probable sources "Messrs Rhea and Bayard" used for compiling the record book were the personal records of the minister and records obtained from parents. Only ten dates of baptism are missing, seven for a single family; forty-six dates of birth are missing. If the original information was obtained from the parents, the ratio of dates of birth remembered to baptismal dates remembered should be greater, primarily because parents would more likely remember when their children were born than when they were baptized. The consistency of the baptismal information suggests that the entries in register were copied from a source maintained by a minister inter-ested in preserving a record of his sacramental acts. The 1769 session records list no sacramental acts. This fact leads to only one conclusion: Rev. Gilbert Tennent kept a personal record, and the pre-1769 baptismal information found in the register of the Second Presbyterian Church in Philadelphia was taken from that record five years after Tennent's death.[31]

Extant records for the Presbyterian Church in Pennsylvania suggest that if an early tradition for keeping records existed, that tradition was the maintenance of personal records rather than church registers. Rev. Jedediah Andrews kept a personal register that was later indentified as a church register. Rev. John Ewing, who served the same congregation, maintained a personal list of baptisms and marriages that was later incorporated into the church register. As noted above, evidence from the Second Presbyterian Church register suggests that Rev. Gilbert Tennent's personal register formed the foundation for a later church record. Personal registers can also be found for other Presbyterian ministers, including Rev. William Marshall, whose personal list of pastoral acts later became the register for Scots Presyterian Church in Philadelphia. The existence of these registers indicates that, in the absence of Presbyterian Church registers, genealogists working on Presbyterian families should first identify the pastor of the church where that ancestor worshipped, and then attempt to track down that pastor's personal register—if one exists.

Genealogists searching for baptismal records must realize that Presbyterian ministers were not the only pastors who maintained personal registers. Similar records were also kept by several Lutheran and Reformed ministers. The personal register of Rev. John Caspar Stoever, already mentioned, contains baptismal records for some of Pennsylvania's earliest Lutheran families. In 1754, Daniel Schumacher (1729–1787) began serving Lutheran congregations in Berks and Lehigh counties. His private register survives, listing over fifteen hundred baptisms that he performed between 1754 and 1774. This register contains some of the earliest baptismal records for these two counties. Volume three of Rev. Muhlenberg's journals lists many baptisms that he performed after retiring in 1777.

Personal registers kept by Reformed pastors include those of Rev. John Conrad Bucher, begun in 1763, and of Rev. John Waldschmidt. Rev. Jacob Lischy, who served Reformed congregations in York County, began a private register in 1745. Charles Glatfelter notes that "[s]ometimes he entered his baptisms in the church register, sometimes in his private register and occasionally in both."[32] But Lischy's entries are not the only instances of double entries. The register for Reed's Lutheran Church in Tulpehocken contains some "backfilled" entries from Rev. Stoever's register. Similarly, baptisms from Rev. Schumacher's private register are listed in the published records of the Jerusalem Lutheran Church, Western Salisbury Township, Lehigh County.

Locating church records is easier than finding ministers' personal registers. Church registers are essentially public records—they are maintained for institutions and, as such, their survival are tied to the survival of the church. If the congregation continues, then the records continue and remain accessible to the public. Personal registers, on the other hand, were private property and probably remained private property. Quite simply, upon the demise of the minister who initiated the record, his personal papers were either passed on to succeeding generations of the minister's heirs or, alternately, became the property of one of the church members. A short history, written on the inside cover of Rev. Jedediah Andrews' register, shows what happened to one personal record. On 16 March 1753, six years after Rev. Andrews died, Edward Shippen, a member of Rev. Andrews' church, saw to it that ". . . this book of records should be preserved," so he directed his ". . . executors and administrators [to] take particular care of it. It was delivered to me [Edward Shippen] by William Gray one of the executors of the Rev. Mr. Jedediah Andrews. dec'd."[33] The whereabouts of the book for the next 56 years is uncertain but, in 1829, James P. Wilson wrote:

"This book was handed over to me about twenty years ago by some person from the Shively family who were Hugenots originally emigrating from France on account of the revocation of the edict of Nantz. I now send it to the Treasurer of the First Presbyterian Church that it may never escape or be loaned to anyone but remain with the records. The 2 vol is in the hands of Mr. Fullerton, the last I have and wish it to be placed with this at my decease.

signed James P. Wilson 29 Jan 1829
depositied in the fire box of the church 2 Feb 1829
by Wm. Davidson Treasuere.[34]

Uncaring or unsuspecting heirs and relatives were not the only vehicles for the loss of private registers. In 1764, Rev. Muhlenberg noted
in his journal that the sermons and books of a minister in Georgia
had gone up for sale at public auction. According to Muhlenberg, the
personal records of the minister were enroute to Georgia and the ship
fell into enemy hands. Privateers eventually recaptured the ship and
its cargo, and the goods, including the ministers personal property,
eventually came to Philadelphia. Muhlenberg further noted that
someone in Philadelphia wanted to purchase the books and records
and send them back to Georgia, but the owners refused.

The Reformed minister, Rev. Michael Schlatter, lost his library and
other personal property during the Revolutionary War. During his
confinement in a Philadelphia jail in 1777, ". . . his dwelling house on
Chestnut-Hill was cruelly plundered by British troops on the fifth of
December."[35] Among the many items taken were more than 800 books,
pictures, and maps; possibly taken or destroyed with them were baptismal records for some of Pennsylvania's earliest German families.

Fortunately for genealogists, not all private registers have been
destroyed. In fact, many have been turned over to libraries and to
public archives, although it is still possible that other early personal
registers are privately held and thus cannot be easily accessed by
public institutions.

Chapter 10

Activities Related to Baptism

Directives to church members in the Anglican *Book of Common Prayer* stated that parents were to notify the minister of the parish prior to bringing an infant to the church for baptism.[1] But prior notification was not limited to the practices of the Church of England; numerous entries in Rev. Muhlenberg's journals indicate that this procedure prevailed in the Lutheran churches as well. It was customary to notify Muhlenberg on a Saturday that the child was ready for baptism the following day. Usually the father of a child approached Rev. Muhlenberg to request the baptism, but several journal entries indicate that occasionally the request may have been made by a midwife. If the family lived a great distance from the church and/or home of the pastor, then they generally arrived early on Sunday morning and notified the minister prior to the worship service.

Emergency baptisms on short notice for a seriously ill or dying infant presented a problem for most ministers, as did the arrival on the minister's doorstep, without prior notice, of parents seeking baptism for their children. These people were often not members of that particular minister's church. For example, the two mothers who showed up at Muhlenberg's house on 9 November 1764 had come ". . . from the ship lying at anchor near the city with their infant children and asked for me to baptize them."[2]

Rev. Muhlenberg does not provide much descriptive detail in his journals about baptismal ceremonies or services. His comments are generally restricted to ". . . had to baptize children in the presence of the congregation."[3] One unusual exception is this entry, dated 31 May 1748, documenting the baptism of a young English woman named Susanna Hopkins, age nineteen. Muhlenberg notes that he had examined her publicly in the presence of the congregation. "After she had clearly and fitly answered all the questions I had her recite the Creed and renounce the devil. Then I called upon the congregation to join in the intercession, commended her to the Triune God in prayer and baptized her using the form."[4]

A more graphic description of a typical eighteenth-century baptism comes to us from the writings of Gottlieb Mittelberger:

> In the rural districts of Pennsylvania the newborn children are not brought to church to receive the holy baptism till they are a fortnight, several weeks, three or six months, and sometimes a whole year old; so that such large and wild children often kick at the preacher or baptist, thus giving rise to laughter. Many Pennsylvanian mothers are in the habit of suckling their unruly babies in church, even during the holy baptism. Many parents act as sponsors for their own children, because they have no faith or confidence in other people in this important point; for which they are not to be blamed, for many a one will not say what he believes.[5]

Understandably, Gottlieb Mittelberger brought a personal bias to his observations based upon his experiences in Germany, where the custom was to baptize children shortly after birth. As has been noted in this text, however, the situation in Pennsylvania was somewhat different. Many children in Pennsylvania were baptized at a later age because parents experienced difficulty finding a minister.

Mittelberger was also witness to the fact that in Pennsylvania many ministers had to take a less rigid approach to the baptismal liturgy—thus permitting parental sponsorship—than in Germany, where sponsors at Lutheran baptisms virtually always held the child. In Pennsylvania, one or both parents may have been raised in the traditions of a different faith, so procedures sometimes varied. It is possible that some parents may merely have preferred the Presbyterian form, wherein they rather than sponsors held the child for baptism.

This easing of traditions was occurring in many eighteenth-century Pennsylvania churches. On 25 March 1778, for example, the pastor of the Swedish Lutheran Church in Philadelphia added this note about a baptism he had performed: "The father being a Presbyterian held the child in his own hands taking the vow all upon himself; but no objection was made to the form and the ceremony of The Church of England."[6]

Not all children were baptized at a Sunday service; many were baptized privately at home. One of the ministers of Old Swedes in Philadelphia recorded in the church register his experience at a private baptism:

> The woman overtook me and Mr. Pearson in our road to Darby yesterday evening desiring that I might come to baptize her child as I had baptized two before and she would have them all three in one book. I told her I would call at the house upon my return this day, and did so accordingly upon which the man put me in the road to Mrs. Cox. John and Lydia Cox, Mary born 23 February baptized March 26, Present the mother and Mrs. Mary Marshall, whose brother is father to the child and spoke Swede to me, from the bed when I saw his sister last Friday. This child was baptized in the house after the service by the person whose hand is above—the ceremony was read in full and in the presence of Mr. Gustavus Risberg and Cap. Samson from Stockholm who obtained his discharge from the obligation he was laid under the other day in the Commissary General's Office in Market Street.
>
> But whilst the persons above mentioned remained in the Common Parlour, a single woman came with a child desiring me to baptize it. I went into the other room and after a few questions sprinkled the child with water without any further ceremony, only I asked the woman the parents name and was told that John and Mary Bridges owned this child, whose name was called Sara, in remembrance of our grandmother buried about a year ago and was born March 2, 1780. Further without

asking I was told that the parents live in one of Joseph Turner's houses and that they had two children baptized by me before.[7]

Use of the term "ownership" as it applies to the baptism of the second child infers that the parents of the infant were probably African American slaves.

Activities related to the baptism of an infant in Pennsylvania were not restricted to the ceremony. Mention is made of ministers attending dinner at the home of the parents after performing the baptism. This fact can be verified in an entry dated 2 August 1778, wherein the minister of Old Swedes Lutheran Church notes in the register that he had baptized a child where he also had dined.[8] Also, on one occasion, Rev. Muhlenberg notes that "widow Anna Agatha Gerstenmayer had brought him wine and cake from yesterday's baptismal dinner at her son-in-law's Christian Dietrich."[9] Baptismal dinners were apparently a custom of the English and Scotch-Irish as well. Mention is made in Muhlenberg's journal of a "christening dinner" for the wife of an Englishman.[10]

A tradition or custom that became associated with baptism in Pennsylvania's German-speaking community was the *Taufschein*— a baptismal certificate embellished with Pennsylvania German folk art. The typical *Taufschein* includes the names of the infant and both parents, the mother's maiden name, the township and county where the birth occurred, the date of baptism, and the names of the pastor and sponsors. Scholars of this Pennsylvania German practice note that the origins for this tradition probably stem from *Taufbrief* or *Gottelbrief*, which were certificates of baptism presented to the child with a gift, generally a coin, at or after the baptism in Germany.[11] In Pennsylvania, the *Taufschein* became associated with baptism in the mid-eighteenth century and later, and has resulted in a body of original records that are probably under-used by genealogists working on early Pennsylvania families.

Money is a subject frequently mentioned in records related to eighteenth-century Pennsylvania baptisms, but based on information available its role cannot be fully understood. Some of the early itinerant ministers working in Pennsylvania prior to the arrival of Rev. Muhlenberg were baptizing infants for a fee. Gottlieb Mittelberger's writings note that ministers around 1754 were paid one dollar for baptizing infants.[12] Because Rev. Muhlenberg did not want to be accused of selling the sacraments of the church, one of his first acts as pastor of the New Hanover Lutheran Church in Montgomery County was to announce before the congregation that church members "were not to pay anything when they had their children baptized . . . [but that] there were other ways to support the pastor."[13] Ministers in the Reformed church were equally sensitive to the issue of money. In 1748 the Coetus of the Reformed Church established fees, but only for performing marriages and preaching sermons; there was no charge for baptisms.[14]

While Rev. Muhlenberg and other ministers did not charge a fee for baptizing infants, they were willing to accept some form of remuneration for their services. For example, many entries in Muhlenberg's journal note the amounts he received from parents (principally the father) when he was approached and asked to baptize an infant. The entry for Saturday, 22 May 1762, is typical: "Nicholas Jacob also reported his child for baptism and gave 2s 6d."[15] The exact nature of these fees is uncertain. Muhlenberg labeled the money that he received as contributions "for salary,"[16] but evidence can be found in other records suggesting that the money was paid to record the baptism: "There was no charge for baptisms, but it became the practice for parents to pay something for entering a baptism in the church register. In 1762 the Philadelphia Reformed [Church] assured that their pastor would receive [£]0.1.0 for each such entry."[17]

Muhlenberg noted in his journal that one minister, Rev. John Helfrich Schaum, was charging one schilling to record baptisms.[18] Pastor Frederick Weiser, in an article on baptism, says that "Pastors did not take fees for baptism. . . . They did take fees, however, for recording baptisms and the going fee appears to have been 7s 6d."Pastor Weiser goes on to note that ". . . even if the fee was not paid the baptism was recorded. . . ."[19] This was certainly the situation with Rev. Muhlenberg, who refused money for baptisms from parents who were poor. But perhaps not all ministers agreed with Muhlenberg's approach; it is possible that some baptisms went unrecorded because poor families could not afford the expense of recordation.

When the father or midwife initially contacted the minister to announce the infant's readiness for baptism, the pastor undoubtedly asked a number of question—including the infant's name and date of birth. After obtaining this information, the minister probably recorded all or part of it. We are left with relevant questions, however, about when and where the information may have been recorded. If the baptism and/or interview took place either in the church or in the pastor's home, then the odds are great that a quill, inkwell, and record book were at hand to enter the record. Of course, if the register were not immediately available, the minister could have written the information on a separate list for later entry—otherwise, he would have had to record it from memory.

In Muhlenberg's case, it appears that the information was recorded upon notification that the parents were ready to have the child baptized. An entry in his journal on Saturday, 9 April 1763, notes: "Late in the evening I meditated a little more and also recorded a number of children who had been announced for baptism tomorrow."[20] Other journal and church register entries confirm that Muhlenberg entered information when he was initially contacted by the father. On 22 October 1763, he wrote in his journal: "Philip Truckenmuller announced his child for baptism tomorrow."[21] Rev. Muhlenberg noted in the next day's entries that he had baptized four children on that Sunday. But strangely, the only recorded baptism in the church register is the one for Johann Georg, son of Joh. Philip and Anna Catharina Truckenmiller, the infant of the man who on Saturday had announced his child for baptism.

An earlier entry in Rev. Muhlenberg's journal indicates that he was not the only pastor who recorded birth and baptismal information when it was first sought. Rev. Handschuh, the assistant pastor at St. Michael's and Zion Lutheran Church in Philadelphia, apparently handled some of his entries in the same manner—recording the information when the father contacted him to announce the child for baptism. On 4 April 4 1762, Rev. Muhlenberg wrote in his journal that he had "baptized three children who had been reported to Handschuh."[22] The three baptisms performed by Muhlenberg on Sunday, 4 April 1762, can be found on the list of baptisms kept by Rev. Handschuh.[23] The inter-related activities of these two Lutheran pastors raises the possibility that it was the custom, as well, for other ministers to record baptismal information when first approached by one or both parents rather than after the fact of baptism.

The recording of baptismal information when the father initially notified the minister was almost mandatory, at least for some pastors. Entries in church registers show that some ministers performed numerous baptisms in a single day. On 15 May 1763, for example, Rev. George Alsentz (1734–1767), pastor of the Reformed Church in Germantown, baptized eight infants.[24] Most ministers probably had more time to record information on Saturdays, for Sundays were chaotic, as is evidenced by one entry in Muhlenberg's journal. On Saturday, 6 August 1763, Rev. Muhlenberg traveled with his family to New Jersey, where German settlers had not had a service since June of 1762. The size of the crowd on the following day gave Muhlenberg cause for concern, as he had to give communion and baptize

> . . . twenty-two infants who had been registered. The church was so crowded . . . and the twenty-two children were crying so loudly the noise was wretched. After I had baptized them all and had dismissed them the mothers hurried with them out in the open air.[25]

It is obvious that no minister under these conditions would have the time or desire to record twenty-two baptisms.

Problems stem from those records in which the minister was called upon to perform an emergency baptism in the home, or from baptisms performed when the minister was preaching at a distant location. In these instances, the pastor had either to record that information on a scrap of paper so that he could later copy that data in the church register, or he could try to record the data based on his memory of the event. As Charles Glatfelter notes in volume two of *Pastors and People*, "[s]ince the baptismal register was usually kept in the church, baptisms performed elsewhere were most likely to go unrecorded."[26] But evidence suggesting that pastors recorded information onto slips of paper and later recopied that data into the church register can be found in a number of places.

The registers of St. Joseph's Catholic Church in show that the priests of the parish recorded information when they went out on their many missions. On 21 April 1765, for example, a priest from St. Joseph's, "while on a mission," baptized four infants at Haycock in Bucks County, Pennsylvania. Another priest performed two baptisms on 18 June 1768 at Reading Furnace in Pennsylvania, and on 19 March 1769, a priest baptized four children at Pilesgrove in Salem County, New Jersey.[27] For this information to have survived, the priest must have recorded that data when the event took place; it is extremely doubtful that he carried a record book from the church on his journeys. First, the weight of the book would have presented a problem and, second, there was always the danger of leaving the book at some distant location or losing it while crossing a river or stream. The priests of St. Joseph's Catholic Church probably took quills and paper or parchment to make notes of their activities and later transfer the information about the baptisms into the church register.

Limited access to a quill and paper meant that when the pastor finally had an opportunity to record the baptism, he was forced to recall the information from memory if he had not kept previous notes. Incomplete baptismal records resulting from a minister's inability to recall every detail of the baptism create a serious problem faced by genealogists when working with Pennsylvania's early registers.

Incomplete records, found in all church registers, should not be confused with irregular records. Irregular records generally occur with a change of pastors—when the format in the register changes to reflect the new minister's recording style. The Germantown Reformed Church register provides a good example. Rev. Christian Faehring (1738–1779) was pastor of the church from 1769 to 1772. His baptismal entries included name of the infant, dates of birth and baptism, names of both parents, and names of the sponsors. Rev. Faehring was followed by Rev. Albert Helffenstein (1748–1790), who recorded the name of the infant, dates of birth and baptism, and the names of both parents only—leaving out the names of sponsors. While a genealogist may view Helffenstein's work as incomplete because he failed to record sponsors' names, the records are not incomplete inasmuch as his pattern of entries is consistent. Purely, it was the style of Rev. Helffenstein not to name the sponsors.

Incomplete records can be defined as entries wherein pertinent information is missing. For example, if the pastor of a church typically enters the name of the infant, the names of parents, dates of birth and baptism, and the names of the sponsors, but one of the above parts is missing, then the genealogist has found an incomplete record. One

representative example can be found in the following entry in the register of the Reformed Church in Germantown: baptized December 12,
1762, _____ son of Johannes Stots and
_____, born _____,
sponsors were the parents.[28] Genealogists working with seemingly
incomplete records are obligated to verify the transcription with the
original, if only to make certain that the entry is actually an incomplete record rather than a bad transcription.

Any one of several pieces of information can be missing from an
incomplete record: the name of the infant, the date of birth or baptism,
or the names of one or both parents. The missing information generally follows a discernible pattern. Most often missing is the date of
birth, followed by the name of the child. Sometimes the mother's
name is omitted as well. The date of baptism and name of the father
are rarely missing for two obvious reasons. The pastor, having pre-
sided at the baptism, was usually able to recall the date of the service;
he also could more easily recall a father's name because the father
(probably a member of the church) was the person most likely to
have contacted him at some earlier time to request the sacrament.

The pattern of missing information is not absolute, however. Incomplete records can be found wherein the names of both parents are
missing, along with the name of the infant and date of birth. Surprisingly, these records may provide names of both sponsors. When recording these entries, the pastor may have been able to recall the
names of the sponsors if he knew them better than the parents. In fact,
the sponsors were possibly members of his church, and the parents
may not have been.

Evidence found in Pennsylvania's church registers shows that the
problem of incomplete records is not limited to a single time period.
The registers of Christ Church for a baptism performed 1 April 1722
provide only skeleton information—the father's name and the date of
baptism.[29] Missing information, of course, would include the date of
birth, name of the infant, and name of the mother.

Incomplete records are not unique to any one church or denomination; they can be found in Reformed, Lutheran, Presbyterian, Episcopalian, and Catholic registers. The pattern of incompleteness affects
all denominations—obviously a factor of human nature or, more

specifically, the inability of any one person to remember pertinent information without having taken notes.

Perhaps the entry for George Rodt's baptism in St. Joseph's Catholic register sums up the problem. That entry contains the following information: George Rodt, son of Thomas and Mary, born 28 September 1778 and baptized 30 October 1778. At the end of this entry, the Catholic priest added the enigmatic comment, "I think."[30]

Chapter 11

Record Problems

The failure of some ministers to recall and record baptismal information is not the sole reason why historians in pursuit of their family history are plagued by missing information. Another source of frustration for genealogists is the persistent and recurring gaps that appear in many early Pennsylvania baptismal registers. Many of those gaps exist because of the pastor competence and availability problem discussed earlier. Other gaps occurred because of the constant turmoil and discord within some congregations, or because of other unusual social or political circumstances in the colonies.

Family historians working with early Pennsylvania registers must be aware that they may encounter such gaps and that these will certainly impact upon their search for family information. A researcher, for example, may find information on some children in a family and not on others. The missing records may, in fact, be considered "lost" only because the children in question were born during a period when the church had no pastor to keep baptismal records. Or, in other instances, the information is not really missing; it may merely be recorded in some unexpected place.

The register of the Germantown Lutheran Church, which contains a gap from 29 November 1777 to 13 July 1778, provides an unusual explanation for apparent missing records. In November of 1777 the pastor of the church, Rev. John Frederick Schmidt (1746–1812), wrote into the register the reason for the existence of a seven months' gap: "the arrival of British troops interrupted the service."[1] Not realizing or considering such extenuating circumstances of the Revolutionary War, historians working on families with children born during the occupation of the City of Philadelphia will have trouble finding data on those families in this and other Philadelphia church records. Heinrich and Barbara Keyser provide a good example of one of those families. Their names appear in the register of the Germantown Lutheran Church with two sons: George, baptized 26 May 1776, and Johannes, baptized 11 February 1782.[2] The register of a different Philadelphia church reveals that this couple were also the parents of a child born and baptized when the city was occupied by the British. When the parents sought baptism for this son, Heinrich, the only available minister was the pastor of the Reformed Church in Germantown, who had remained in the city throughout the occupation.[3] As a result, the baptismal record for this one child of a Lutheran family appears in the Germantown Reformed Church register.

The circumstances affecting the baptism for one of the Keyser children does not represent an isolated incident. The basic causes may differ—merely the absence of a Lutheran minister, for example, rather than the political upheaval of the Revolutionary War as in the previous example—but other baptismal accounts can also be found in unexpected locations. So-called "missing" baptismal information can often be recovered from another church register.

The inability of many rural congregations to attract and keep ministers meant that some churches lay dormant for extended periods of time. This unfortunate circumstance resulted in matching extended periods of time when no baptismal information was recorded. The register of Millbach Reformed Church in Lebanon County is typical. For eleven years, from 1782 until 1793, this congregation was without the services of a pastor— resulting in a fairly sizable gap in that baptismal register. A similar two-year gap in the register of the Jerusalem Lutheran Church in Lehigh County stems from the fact that this church had no pastor from October 1763 until February 1766.[4] The Tohickon Lutheran congregation in Bucks County was without a pastor for more than two years, the result being a gap in that register from 21

April 1757 to 8 December 1760.[5] Several gaps can also be found in the register of the New Goshenhoppen Reformed Church in Montgomery County because of difficulties that congregation had in getting pastors.[6]

Lutheran and Reformed church records are not the only church registers reflecting the problem of long periods without baptismal notations. A gap lasting several years can be found in the registers of the Second Presbyterian Church in Philadelphia, and two early gaps exist in the records of Christ Church, again in Philadelphia.[7] An eleven-year gap from 1747 to 1758 appears in the registers of the Goshenhoppen Catholic Church in Berks County.[8]

Gaps in church registers and their importance to genealogical research can be graphically illustrated by constructing a profile depicting the number of baptisms recorded annually in a church record. This profile is constructed by counting the number of baptisms performed each calendar year and comparing the annual total of baptisms recorded. The chart below for the Jerusalem Lutheran Church in Lehigh County for the years 1755 through 1769 illustrates how this kind of chart can be constructed.

Jerusalem/Schmaltzgass Lutheran Church Lehigh County		
	Year	Baptisms
Daniel Schumacher (served 1758–1763)		
(the first entry was recorded 1 January 1759)	1759	17
	1760	14
	1761	18
	1762	12
(the last entry was recorded 16 October 1763)	1763	11
	1764	0
	1765	0
Daniel Schumacher (served 1766–1768)		
(the first entry was recorded 2 February 1766)	1766	11
	1767	7
(the last entry was recorded 18 December 1768)	1768	9
Jacob Van Buskirk (served 1769–1793)		
(first entry recorded on 5 November 1769)	1769	1

This profile of baptisms reveals that the Jerusalem Lutheran Church was a small congregation, and the number of baptisms per year ranged from a low of seven in 1767 to a high of eighteen in 1761. Also apparent is the gap from 16 October 1763 to 2 February 1766. Genealogists researching families with children born in 1764 and 1765 and expecting to find Jerusalem Lutheran Church baptismal information about those children can anticipate problems. Consider the family of Jacob and Agnes Sauerwein. Three of their children were baptized by the minister of Jerusalem Lutheran Church: Johan Jacob, bp. 26 July 1761; Jurg Adam, bp. 26 June 1763; and Catharina, bp. July 3, 1768.[9] The spacing of baptisms for these children suggests that an additional child or children could have been born when the church was without the sevices of a minister. Skepticism and persistence in this case pays off! A baptismal record in another Lehigh County church register confirms that observation. The baptism of John Sauerwein, born 5 November 1765, appears in the register of Zion Reformed Church in Allentown. He was born 14 October 1765, and the Zion Reformed record lists the parents as Jacob and Agnes Sauerwein.[10]

Construction of this profile for the Jerusalem Lutheran Church helps anyone researching this family to understand two things: one, the absence of information for the years 1764 and 1765 is a signal to search for alternative sources; and two, the stray baptism in another church record for this family cannot be taken to mean that the parents had relocated and joined a new church.

Most gaps is church records are fairly obvious, and genealogists working with records where they exist know that these gaps indicate that some information is probably missing. But registers wherein a pastor may have recorded some—but not necessarily all—of baptisms he performed present another obstacle to research. Profiles of baptismal registers are especially useful in helping to identify records where researchers encounter this problem. Consider the example at the top of the next page.

The profile of baptisms for the Lower Saucon Reformed Church in Northampton County shows that this church was a small congregation served by three ministers over a period of approximately fifteen years. The range of baptisms from a low of seven in 1790 to a high of thirty-six in 1792 is considerable, and this profile should alert reseach-

Reformed Church, Lower Saucon Township Northampton County		
	Year	Baptisms
Casper Wack (served 1781–1786)		
	1785	29
	1786	16
Herman Wynckhaus (served 1786–1790)		
	1787	24
	1788	14
	1789	13
	1790	7
	1791	7
John Mann (served 1791–ca. 1795–96)		
	1792	36
	1793	34
	1794	19
	1795	8

ers working on families with children baptized at this church to expect problems in their research for the years 1790 and 1791, and again in 1795.

Baptismal information on the family of Andreas and Christina Brunner abstracted from this profile assures the necessity to explore alternate informational sources for problem years. Four children were born to this couple between 1785 to 1795: Heinrich, b. 19 August 1785, bp. 23 October 1785; Magdalena, b. 31 July 1787, bp. 19 September 1787; Christina, b. 27 May 1792, bp. 4 May 1792; and Anna Margaretha, b. 7 February 1795, bp. 10 February 1795.[11] The spacing of births for this family suggests a possibility that Andreas and Christina Brunner may have had an additional child born in 1789 or 1790. Matching a profile of known births for this couple with a profile of baptismal records for their church reveals that, indeed, few baptisms were recorded in the church register during the years when this couple possibly or probably had more children.

A birth or baptismal record to confirm this observation could not be found in any nearby church register for an additional Brunner child. In this case, a *Taufschein*, a personal baptismal record common to early families of German heritage, provided the crucial key element.

This *Taufschein* reads: "For Maria Eva, daughter of Andreas and Christina (Gangawehr) Brunner, born February 25, 1789, 9 p.m., in Virgo, in Lower Saucon Township, Northampton County, baptized by Pastor Winckhaus. Sponsor Maria Eva Mohr."12 Where this Brunner family is concerned, the profile of the Lower Saucon Reformed Church record, combined with a profile of birth records for this family, plus a third factor—a *Taufschein*—completes the puzzle.

Genealogists also must deal with the problem of misplaced information—that is, family data recorded in an unexpected location—for reasons beyond those of an absent or negligent church minister. The frequent mention of place names in some early Pennsylvania church registers conclusively illustrates that children were not always baptized where the parents lived or attended church. For any number of reasons they went elsewhere, and depending on the circumstances surrounding the baptism, the information may have been recorded in an unexpected location.

The baptismal record for James Boyd found in the register of the Scots Prebysterian Church in Philadelphia provides an interesting example:

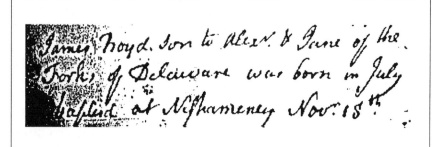

On Thursday, 18 November 1773, the pastor of Scots Presbyterian happened to be in Neshaminy, Bucks County, where he performed the baptism. His entry in the Philadelphia record notes that James, son of Alexander and Jane Boyd "of the Forks of the Delaware," was born in July 1773.[13] In this instance, three locations are involved: James Boyd was born in Northampton County; he was baptized in Bucks County; and his baptism was recorded in Philadelphia.

A similarly interesting case is that of the Honig/Henigs families, among the early settlers in upper Bucks County. Baptismal records for several children with this surname can be found in the register of the Tohickon Reformed Church, but no records for Jacob and Catharine Honig's children can be found there or, in fact, in any other Bucks County church registers. The register of the Goshenhoppen Catholic Church in Berks County, however, lists information for Maria Salome, baptized 18 August 1765, and Elizabeth, born 13 September 1767.[14] A record for the third daughter, Mary Magdalena, born 14 February 1770, appears in the register of St. Joseph's Catholic Church in Philadelphia.[15] The Honigs did not travel either to Philadelphia or Goshenhoppen to have their daughters baptized. In each instance, the priest noted having baptized the children at Haycock in Bucks County. These extant records confirm that the ceremonies, although performed where the family lived, were recorded elsewhere.

Rev. Muhlenberg entered into the church register of St. Michael's and Zion Lutheran Church, Philadelphia, a record for the baptisms of two children he had baptized on 15 August 1774 at Pikestown in Chester County.[16] Muhlenberg's journal entry for Monday, 15 August 1774, reveals his visit to Pikestown to lay the corner stone for the new Lutheran church building:

> Several deacons of Pikestown came to meet us [in Providence, Montgomery County] and showed us the most convient route to drive our coach through the woods and across the Schuylkill River. Arriving at the church at Pikestown we found a large crowd of people both German and English.[17]

Muhlenberg's record goes on to provide a fairly detailed description of the ceremony.

The two children baptized were Johann Heinrich, son of Johann Gottlieb and Louisa Eberle, and Elisabeth, daughter of Michael and Susanna Heilman.[18] Genealogists working on these two families would miss valuable family information if they limited their search to Chester County church records; they would miss not only the names of the two children, but also some very interesting historical detail about events of the day these two infants were baptized.

Historians researching early New Jersey families should spend time working with Pennsylvania's church registers on the chance that baptismal information for some of their ancestors might have been recorded across the Delaware River. For example, the pastor of the Swedish Lutheran Church in Philadelphia baptized eight children of the Steelman family and three children of the Lee family in Egg Harbor, New Jersey, on 17 May 1765.[19] At Ringwood in Passaic County, New Jersey, on 31 May 1772, the priest of St. Joseph's Catholic Chuch in Philadelphia baptized five children and, on 26 August 1773 he baptized seven more children—all in Burlington County, New Jersey.[20] Other New Jersey place names mentioned in this register include Pilesgrove in Salem County, and Bacon Ridge in Somerset County. Baptismal records for children baptized at each of these locations can be found in the Philadelphia church registers.

The reasons why baptisms were recorded in a variety of locations are probably as varied as the families themselves. The persistent difficulty experienced by the many congregations in securing pastors was certainly part of the problem—an especially acute problem for Reformed and Lutheran congregations. In 1776, three hundred forty-eight Lutheran and Reformed congregations were served by eighty-two ministers.[21] The experiences of Rev. John Conrad Bucher (1730–1780) and Rev. John Lewis Voigt (1731–1800) are typical. Rev. Bucher simultaneously served five Reformed congregations in Lebanon County from 1770 to 1780: Jonestown; Hill or Quittophilla; Kimmerlings; Fredericksburg; and Lebanon. Similarly, Rev. Voigt simultaneously served five Lutheran congregations in Montgomery and Chester counties from 1772 to 1777: New Hanover; Providence; Pottstown; Pikeland; and Pikestown.[22] In contrast, the Presbyterians had forty-eight pastors serving one hundred twelve congregations in 1776 while, at approximately the same time, the Church of England had ten clerics serving twenty congregations. On average, then, one Lutheran or Reformed minister served four congregations; his Presbyterian or Anglican counterpart was generally required to cover only two.[23]

The simultaneous or concurrent service of many pastors, particularly in Pennsylvania's rural areas, resulted in the recordation of baptismal information in registers different from where the family may have worshiped or lived. The register of the Tohickon Reformed Church in Bucks County offers one example. A profile of the baptis-

	Year	Baptisms
Tohickon Reformed Church		
Bucks County		
Jacob Reiss (served 1749–1756)		
(entries 27 August 1749 to December 1749)	1749	9
	1750	23
	1751	35
	1752	20
	1753	24
	1754	36
	1755	10
	1756	33
Egidius Hecker (served 1756–1762)		
	1757	126
	1758	121
	1759	122
	1760	86
	1761	90
(last entry recorded 8 February 1762)		
(17 February 1763)	1763	1
	1764	0
	1765	0
(12 October 1766)	1766	6

register for that congregation (above) illustrates the problem.

This profile shows a surge in baptisms from 1757 through 1761. In 1756 the total number of baptisms was thirty-three. The following year, that number jumped to one hundred twenty-six—and a similar level of baptisms was maintained for several years. All of these baptisms were performed and/or were recorded by Rev. Egidius Hecker (1726–1794), pastor of this congregation from 1756 until 1762. During this time period, Rev. Hecker actually served three congregations: Tohickon Reformed in Bucks County, Lower Saucon Reformed in Northampton County, and Upper Milford Reformed in Lehigh County. The presence of many Northampton County and Lehigh County family names—including Lerch, Frutschy, Frantz, Bruch, Dreisbach, Schweitzer, Van Etten, Dornblaser, Mohr, Eberhard, Schoner, and others—is convincing evidence that baptisms for families in Northampton and Lehigh counties were recorded in the Bucks County register.

The foregoing Tohickon Reformed Church profile, when compared with a second (Lutheran) congregational record, reveals another unexpected possibility. The dramatic jump in baptisms under Rev. Hecker reflects not only the likelihood that he recorded baptisms for infants from adjacent counties, but that he also recorded baptisms for families belonging to other denominations. An analysis of the register for the Tohickon Lutheran Church lists only two baptisms from 1757 to 1761. This fact suggests a strong probability that a number of the entries in Rev. Hecker's Reformed register may also include baptisms of children whose parents were members of the local Lutheran church.

Rev. Hecker, however, was not the only pastor who recorded information from several congregations in a single register. Researchers will find that other ministers who concurrently served several mid-eighteenth-century Pennsylvania church congregations recorded baptisms in locations other than where that family may have regularly worshipped. As a result, smart genealogists searching for "misplaced" information on Pennsylvania's early families should, first, strive to identify the pastor of the church where their ancestors' children were baptized and, second, track down and thorougly search each and every register where that pastor served—as well as the registers of neighboring congregations.

Chapter 12

Additional Considerations

As already noted in this text, family historians experience difficulty locating baptismal records for any number of reasons: record books were unavailable, records have been lost over the years, eighteenth-century churches had problems securing pastors, and so on. While the numbers of unrecorded baptisms will never actually be confirmed, some miscellaneous surviving records provide hints about the extent of the problem.

The experience of Rev. Charles Beatty may be typical of some other ministers. In 1743 Beatty was ordained as a Presbyterian minister and served as the pastor of the Neshaminy Presbyterian Church in Bucks County from that year until 1772. In 1766 he traveled to the "Ohio Country" to preach to Indians and their neighbors. Rev. Beatty's daily journal of his two-months' journey, eventually published in England, mentions that in the course of his travels he had baptized a number of children. On 26 August 1766, he notes that he had arrived at the home of Andrew Bratton in a location that is the present township of Bratton, Mifflin County, Pennsylvania. Rev. Beatty remarked that on that day he "preached to a Considerable number of People who were very attentive. Baptised 3 Children."[1] The next day's entry notes that he "Baptized a child who was brought to my lodging. . . ," and later that same day he baptized four additional children.[2]

Rev. Beatty specifically mentions at least ten baptisms he performed while on this journey. He obviously had a quill and paper or he could not have maintained the journal, but he never recorded therein any of the children's names. His reason remains a mystery. The areas where he journeyed were sparsely populated, meaning that there were no organized churches with their own record books. Other than the mention of these anonymous baptisms in Beatty's journal, nothing survives in recorded form that can be used for researching these frontier families.

Almost thirty years later, a Presbyterian minister in Chester County, Pennsylvania, entered in the register of the Faggs Manor Presbyterian Church, "April 22, [1792,] baptized eleven children in West Nottingham."[3] No names were given. Again, this minister must have had a quill and record book available, but he neglected to specifically document these baptismal events.

In September of 1780, the pastor of the Swedish Lutheran Church in Philadelphia wrote into the register of that church: "In these records to the best of my knowledge are left out two children baptized lately in the little house opposite Mr. Matthew Johns. . . ."[4] Though he calls attention to the omissions, he fails to provide the missing names.

Rev. Muhlenberg's journal frequently notes the number of children baptized on a given day. A typical entry reads: ". . . early in the morning six fathers announced their children for baptism."[5] Muhlenberg went on to note that he baptized the six children in the forenoon and an additional child, the son of Johannes Weismann, in the evening. Between 30 September 1764 and 11 November 1764, Rev. Muhlenberg's journal notes the baptism of an anonymous thirty-five children.[6] Throughout this period of time, Muhlenberg was the sole pastor of St. Michael's and Zion Lutheran Church in Philadelphia. The records of that church list only twenty-two baptisms. Unfortunately, thirteen baptisms—or approximately one-third of the number mentioned in Muhlenberg's journals—were never recorded in the St. Michael's and Zion register.

Arguably, this is not a significant statistical sample, and it occurred during a period of time when Muhlenberg was overwhelmed with the duties of his congregation following the death of his colleague, Rev. Handschuh. But it illustrates that even a pastor who left an amazingly extensive set of records was so distracted or pressed for time that he failed to record each and every pastoral act.

The precise numbers of baptisms administered by colonial pastors will never be known with certainty, but one surviving record provides additional insight. It concerns a minister who arrived on 9 July 1763 at a Moravian settlement in Bethabara, North Carolina, seeking treatment for his chronic diarrhea. Rev. MacDowell, an Anglican cleric from Braunschweig on Cape Fear River in North Carolina, stayed with the Moravians until September 1763. The Moravian records note: "The English minister held service and preached only once in our Saal [meeting room], and during his soujourn here he baptised 150 of the older and younger children of our neighbors either in our Saal or in his room."[7]

The Moravian entry suggests that this one Anglican minister averaged seventy-five baptisms in his two months' stay. If that average held true over the course of one year, then Rev. MacDowell baptized approximately 900 infants, children, and adults. These projected numbers are probably an abberation, of course. Rev. MacDowell had traveled to a recently settled area of North Carolina where there were no other Anglican pastors. Without question, like many colonial clergy, he baptized quite a few infants in the course of a year. But the question for genealogists becomes: How many baptisms of all religious denominations in eighteenth-century Pennsylvania were never recorded? We will never know.

Another factor contributing to the absence of baptismal records for an untold number of Pennsylvania's early settlers is the fact that many of those pioneers were baptized under emergency circumstances. Many parents, faced with the prospect of imminent death at the hands of attacking Indians, probably baptized their own children in their cabins during the French and Indian War. Verification for this kind of lay baptism resulting from political upheaval and its concomitant trauma can be found in Muhlenberg's 1763 journal entry: ". . . a woman complained of pangs of conscience because during the flight from Indians she had permitted her child to be baptized by a Godless man who gave himself out as a preacher."[8] Other parents facing the death of a child or infant, perhaps out of sheer frustration, baptized that child, thinking, "Even if I cannot help you now, I can at least prepare you for the hereafter."

Not all of those children died. Some survived, were later married, and became parents themselves. History possibly repeated itself as these pioneers moved westward and faced similar situations in the frontier settlements of Ohio or Indiana. Present-day descendants are now frustrated in their search for non-existant baptismal records of these eighteenth-century Pennsylvania ancestors.

Some early lay baptisms, however, can be traced. One recorded emergency baptism was performed 20 February 1761 by Johannes Bender. On that day, Bender lost his wife Elisabeth in childbirth. Apparently the infant was also in danger of dying, because the distraut father performed lay baptism for the infant. The infant survived, and the pastor of St. Michael's and Zion Lutheran Church left a record, dated 1 March 1761, confirming this baptism.[9] Similar records can be found in Catholic registers, but information on emergency baptisms was recorded only in those instances where a priest or pastor was available to perform the proper religious ceremony and/or confirm the initial baptism. How many times did a similar situation take place wherein a problem birth resulted in an emergency baptism performed by the father or midwife—and was never recorded? We will never know.

Finally, some family historians experience difficulty finding baptismal information because their ancestors were not sufficiently committed to any church and, thus, did not take the initiative in having their children baptized. Evidence that some of Pennsylvania's early settlers exercised their newly-found religious freedom can be found in this observation that Gottlieb Mittelberger made during his brief stay in Pennsylvania from 1750 to 1754:

> Others who are themselves baptized, nevertheless do not have their children baptized. When one asks them why, they answer: they neither see nor feel any difference between baptized and unbaptized young people. Also, that nobody keeps his baptismal vows and that it is not necessary to pay the minister a thaler for the ceremony. In my school in Pennsylvania I encountered many adults of both sexes who, when asked whether they were baptized, answered: "No, what is the use of it?"[10]

Rev. Muhlenberg frequently made note in his journal of people who were "negligent" of baptismal rites. In October 1751, he was called to administer baptism to a Pennsylvania-born elderly "Dutchman" facing death. On his deathbed, the man called his children and told them, "I have neglected you and never have instructed you in the way of salvation and baptism."[11] On another occasion, at the time he was instructing a young man born in Pennsylvania in the 1730s, Muhlenberg asked the boy's father why he did had not had his son baptized in infancy. The father replied,

> ". . . there were so many sects in this country he did not know which was best." He himself had been baptized in his infancy in the Dutch Reformed Church but he had not been instructed afterwards consequently he had not known of what advantage baptism had been to him. For this reason he had waited until his children had reached the age of understanding when they could read the Bible for themselves. . . .[12]

Genealogists searching for eighteenth-century ancestral information, at some point, consider two important points. First, one cannot assume that an expected baptism, in fact, ever took place. Second, it must be understood and accepted that, for a variety of reasons, numerous baptisms throughout the entire colonial period in Pennsylvania and elsewhere were never recorded. Some ministers—like Rev. Beatty—had access to a quill and parchment, yet chose to leave no records. Other ministers—like Rev. Muhlenberg—who kept meticulous records, did not always follow through with a written notation following each and every baptism. And then, of course, there were the emergency baptisms performed by parents and midwives but never recorded. Finally, some parents chose not to have their children baptized.

How many eighteenth-century Pennsylvania baptisms were never recorded? Who were the persons involved? We will never know.

Notes

Chapter 2: Baptismal Records, pages 5–12

1. *The Mennonite Encyclopedia: A Comprehensive Reference Work on the Anabaptist-Mennonite Movement* (Scottdale, Pa., 1955), 1: 601.
2. David E. Gardner and Frank Smith, *Genealogical Research in England and Wales* (Salt Lake City, 1956), 1: 156.
3. Milton Rubincam, ed., *Genealogical Research: Methods and Sources* (Washington, D.C., 1980), 1: 480.
4. David Hey, *The Oxford Guide To Family History* (New York, 1993), 190–91.
5. J. Moss Ives, *The Ark and the Dove: The Beginnings of Civil and Religious Liberties in America* (New York, 1936), 3, 16.
6. *New Catholic Encyclopedia* (Washington, D.C., 1980), 9: 401.
7. Hey, 191.
8. Helen Huchinson Woodroofe, "A Chronological List of Philadelphia Churches and Cemeteries, 1642–1790," *Pennsylvania Genealogical Magazine* 30 (1978): 159.
9. Joseph L. Kirlin, *Catholicity in Philadelphia, From the Earliest Missionaries Down to the Present Time* (Philadelphia, 1909), 94.
10. *The Goshenhoppen Registers, 1741–1819: Registers of Baptisms, Marriages, and Deaths of the Catholic Mission at Goshenhoppen* . . . (Baltimore, 1984), 1: note to the reader; hereafter cited as *Goshenhoppen Registers.*
11. The three pre-1760 registers are those of Abington Presbyterian (Montgomery Co.) and the First Presbyterian and Second Presbyterian churches of Philadelphia.
12. *The Statutes of the Realm, Printed by Command of His Majesty King George the Third, From Original Records and Authentic Manuscripts* (Buffalo, 1993), 5: 516.
13. Ibid., 5: 648.
14. Ibid., 5: 364.
15. Adelaide L. Fries, trans., *Records of the Moravians in North Carolina* (Raleigh, 1968), 1: 23–25.

Chapter 3: The Base Position, pages 13–24

1. *New Catholic Encyclopedia,* 2: 54.
2. Ibid., 2: 65
3. Ibid., 3: 238.

4. Paul Johnson, *A History of Christianity* (New York, 1977), 80.
5. Joseph H. Lynch, *Godparents and Kinship in Early Medieval Europe* (Princeton, N.J., 1986), 118–19.
6. *New Catholic Encyclopedia*, 3: 240.
7. Lynch, 121–22.
8. Will Durant, *The Story of Civilization, Part IV, The Age of Faith . . .* (New York, 1950), 738.
9. Julius Bodensieck, ed., *The Encyclopedia of the Lutheran Church* (Minneapolis, 1965), 1: 572–73.
10. *New Catholic Encyclopedia*, 4: 147.
11. Joachim Jeremias, *The Origins of Infant Baptism . . .* (Naperville, Ill., n.d.), 30.
12. Durant, 4: 739.
13. Lynch, 83.
14. Ibid., 293.
15. Jeremias, 29–30.
16. Lynch, 125.
17. Ibid., 144, 277, 279.
18. Ibid., 122–23, 304.
19. Ibid., 405.
20. Barbara A. Hanawalt, *Growing Up in Medieval London . . .* (New York, 1993), 44.
21. John Henry Blunt, ed., *The Annotated Book of Common Prayer . . .* (New York, 1903), 423.
22. Hanawalt, 45.
23. Blunt, 402.
24. Ibid.
25. Hanawalt, 45.
26. Philippe Aries and Georges Duby, *A History of Private Life. . .* (Cambridge, Mass., 1989), 3: 82.
27. Lynch, 251, 279.
28. Hanawalt, 45–46.
29. *New Catholic Encyclopedia* 2: 63, 2: 66.
30. Ibid., 2: 67.
31. Lynch, 24.
32. *New Catholic Encyclopedia*, 2: 66.
33. *Goshenhoppen Registers*, 31.
34. Ibid., 35.
35. Old St. Joseph's Catholic Church, Philadelphia, Baptisms; hereafter cited as Old St. Joseph's Catholic.
36. *New Catholic Encyclopedia*, 2: 66.
37. *Goshenhoppen Registers*, 79.
38. Old St. Joseph's Catholic.
39. *New Catholic Encyclopedia*, 2: 66.
40. Bodensieck, 1: 572–73.
41. *New Catholic Encyclopedia*, 2: 151.

Chapter 4: First Removed, pages 25–44

1. Robert H. Fischer, trans., *The Large Catehchism of Martin Luther* (Philadelphia, 1959), 83.
2. Bodensieck, 1: 183.
3. Ibid.
4. Joel W. Lundeen, ed., *Luther's Works* (Philadelphia, 1986), 53: 102.
5. Ibid., 45: 8.

6. Ibid., 50: 13.

7. Bodensieck, 1: 573.

8. Theodore G. Tappart and John W. Doberstein, trans., *The Journals of Henry Melchior Muhlenberg* (Philadelphia, 1942), 2: 70; hereafter cited as Tappart and Doberstein.

9. Gloria Dei (Old Swedes) Lutheran Church, Philadelphia,Baptisms; hereafter cited as Gloria Dei.

10. Tappart and Doberstein, 1: 624.

11. St. Michael's and Zion Evangelical Lutheran Church, Philadelphia, Baptisms; hereafter cited as St. Michael's and Zion.

12. Charles H. Glatfelter, *Pastors and People: German Lutheran and Reformed Churches in the Pennsylvania Field, 1717–1793, Volume II: The History* (Breiningsville, Pa., 1981), 2: 450.

13. St. Michael's and Zion.

14. Ibid.

15. Glatfelter, 2: 266.

16. Blunt, 407.

17. Ibid., 410.

18. Ibid., 408.

19. Ibid.

20. Ibid., 404.

21. Ibid., 423.

22. Ibid., 408.

23. Ibid., 515.

24. Ibid., 438.

25. Tappart and Doberstein, 1: 355.

26. Sir Robert Phillimore, ed., *The Ecclesiastical Law of the Church of England* (London, 1895), 496.

27. Robert W. Pritchard, *A History of the Episcopal Church* (Harrisburg, Pa., 1991), 74.

28. Glatfelter, 2: 351.

29. William B. Sprague, *Annals of the American Pulpit* (New York, 1969), 5: 280.

30. Joseph Mortimer Levering, *A History of Bethlehem, Pennsylvania, 1741–1892* . . . (Bethlehem, Pa., 1903), 9, 15, 19.

31. Carl John Helmich, "Infant Baptism in the Moravian Church: A Study of Doctrine and Liturgy" (Bethlehem, 1957), 41.

32. *The Book of Order of the Moravian Church in America (Unitas Fratrum), Northern Province* (Bethlehem, 1911), 123; hereafter cited as *Moravian Book of Order*.

33. Helmich, 59.

34. Kenneth G. Hamilton, trans., *The Bethlehem Diary, Volume I: 1742–1744* (Bethlehem, 1971), 1: 33.

35. Fries, 3: 1013.

36. Ibid., 3: 1013–14.

37. *Moravian Book of Order*, 123.

38. Helmich, 59.

39. *A Concise Historical Account of the Present Constitution of the Protestant Church of the United Brethren* . . . (Manchester, England, 1815), Sec. 9.

40. Beverly Prior Smaby, *The Transformation of Moravian Bethlehem from Communal Mission to Family Economy* (Philadelphia, 1988), 23–24.

41. Fries, 4: 829, 2: 545. It also must be noted that the organizational structure of the Moravian Church in the mid-eighteenth century was such that some women held the position of elder. One in particular was Anna Nitschmann (1715–1801). In her capacity as elder, Nitschmann confirmed candidates for communion—making her probably the first woman in America to perform this office.

42. Birth and Baptismal Register for the [Moravian] Congregation, Salisbury, entry 30.

43. Ibid., entry 332.
44. Emory Stevens Bucke, ed., *The History of American Methodism*, (New York, 1964), 29.
45. *New Catholic Encyclopedia*, 9: 735.
46. Sprague, xiii.
47. *Doctrines and Discipline of the Methodist Church* (New York, 1939), 77.
48. Ibid., 54.
49. Bucke, 221.

Chapter 5: The Reformed Position, pages 45–58

1. *The Constitution of the Presbyterian Church (U.S.A.), Part II: Book of Order* (Louisville, 1992), 2: W–2.3000; hereafter cited as *Presbyterian Church Constitution*.
2. Menno Borduin, *Form of Baptism Explained* (Grand Rapids, 1935), 16.
3. *New Catholic Encyclopedia*, 2: 70
4. Will Durant, *The Story of Civilization, Part VI, The Reformation* . . . (New York, 1947), 464.
5. Ibid.
6. Felix B. Gear, *Our Presbyterian Belief* (Atlanta, 1980), 70–71.
7. Lynch, 52.
8. *Presbyterian Church Constitution*, 2: W–2.3011.
9. Guy Soulliard Klett, *Presbyterians in Colonial Pennsylvania* (Philadelphia, 1937), 94; hereafter cited as Klett, *Colonial Pennsylvania*.
10. Rev. John Carmichael, personal register.
11. *Presbyterian Church Constitution*, 2: G–5.000.
12. Bodensieck, 1: 185.
13. Durant, 6: 464.
14. Klett, *Colonial Pennsylvania*, 117–18.
15. Tinicum Presbyterian Church, Red Hill [Bucks Co.], Congregational Records; hereafter cited as Tinicum Presbyterian.
16. Ibid.
17. Presbyterian Church, Oxford [Chester Co.] Session Minutes.
18. Guy Soulliard Klett, *Minutes of the Presbyterian Church in America 1706–1788* (Philadelphia, Pa., 1976), 421; hereafter cited as Klett, *Minutes*.
19. Carmichael, personal register.
20. Ibid.
21. Tinicum Presbyterian.
22. Rev. Jedediah Andrews, personal records.
23. Tinicum Presbyterian.
24. Richard T. Schellhase, "The Reformed Church In The United States," 2.
25. Ibid.
26. Durant, 6: 408.
27. *The Heidelberg Catechism* . . . *in Christian Doctrine* . . . *Churches and Schools of the Palatinate and Elsewhere* (Chambersburg, Pa., 1854), 121.
28. Ibid., question 74.
29. *The Heidelberg Catechish* . . . *of the German Reformed Church in the United States of America* (Chambersburg, Pa., 1841), 86; hereafter cited as *Heidelberg* . . . *German Reformed*.
30. Schellhase, 2.
31. William J. Hinke, *Minutes and Letters of the Coetus of the German Reformed Congregations in Pennsylvania, 1747–1792* . . . (Philadelphia, 1903), 42; hereafter cited as Hinke, *Coetus*.

32. Ibid., 128.
33. Durant, 6: 408.
34. Glatfelter, 2: 251.
35. William J. Hinke, *Early History of the Reformed Church in Pennsylvania* (Reading, Pa., 1906), 50.
36. Ibid., 55.
37. *Heidelberg . . . German Reformed*, 86.
38. *Constitution and Discipline of the German Reformed Church . . .* (Chambersburg, Pa., 1828), article 4.
39. Helen Hutchison Woodroofe, "Baptisms from the Church Book of the German Reformed Church of Philadelphia . . . ," *Pennsylvania Genealogical Magazine* 35 (1987): 9–16.
40. Sprague, 9: 221.
41. Donald K. McKim, ed., *Encyclopedia of the Reformed Faith* (Louisville, 1992), 111.
42. Sprague, 3: 226.
43. *Collections of The New York Genealogical and Biographical Society* (New York, 1928), 8: 87.
44. Apparently this policy changed in the nineteenth century, as witness names are no longer given in the registers.
45. *Collections of The New York Genealogical and Biographical Society*, 8: 96.
46. Rubincam, 1: 248.
47. *Collections of The New York Genealogical and Biographical Society*, 8: 96.

Chapter 6: Anabaptist and Baptist Traditions, pages 59–68

1. *Mennonite Encyclopedia*, 1: 225.
2. William Cathcart, ed., *The Baptist Encyclopedia* (Philadelphia, 1881), 69.
3. Donald F. Durnbaugh, ed, *The Brethren Encyclopedia* (Philadelphia, 1983), 21.
4. Durant, 4: 214.
5. Euan Cameron, *The European Reformation*, (Oxford, England, 1991), 321.
6. H. Frank Eshleman, *Historical Background And Annals Of The Swiss and German Pioneers of Southeastern Pennsylvania . . .* (Lancaster, Pa., 1917), 33.
7. Durant, 4: 397.
8. *Mennonite Encyclopedia*, 1: 225.
9. Ibid.
10. Eshleman, 209.
11. *Mennonite Encyclopedia*, 1: 601.
12. Ibid.
13. *New Catholic Encyclopedia*, 1: 447–48.
14. *Mennonite Encyclopedia*, 1: 90.
15. Ibid., 1: 90.
16. Stephen Scott, *The Amish Wedding and Other Special Occassions . . .* (Intercourse, Pa., 1988), 6.
17. Ibid., 42.
18. *Mennonite Encyclopedia*, 1: 228.
19. H. Leon McBeth, *The Baptist Heritage*, (Nashville, 1987), 144.
20. *Mennonite Encyclopedia*, 1: 228.
21. Cathcart, 69.
22. *Mennonite Encyclopedia* 1: 229.
23. McBeth, 144.
24. Ibid.
25. Pennypack Baptist Church, Philadelphia Co., Baptisms.

26. First Baptist Church, Philadelphia, Baptisms.
27. *Mennonite Encyclopedia* 1: 421.
28. Durnbaugh, 1: 21.
29. Ibid., 1: 83.
30. *Mennonite Encyclopedia* 1: 422.
31. Ibid.
32. Frederic Klees, *The Pennsylvania Dutch* (New York, 1950), 62.

Chapter 7: The Religious Society of Friends, pages 69–82

1. Wilmer A. Cooper, *A Living Faith, An Historical Study of Quaker Beliefs*, (Richmond, Ind., 1990), 91.
2. William C. Braithwaite, *The Beginnings of Quakerism*, (London, 1912), 139.
3. David Hackett Fischer, *Albion's Seed: Four Birtish Folkways in America*, (New York, 1989), 426.
4. Ibid., 427.
5. Ellen Thomas Berry and David Allen, *Our Quaker Ancestors*, (Baltimore, 1987), 27–34.
6. Braithwaite, 313.
7. Ibid., 328.
8. Chester County Friends Monthly Meeting Records.
9. Braithwaite, 139.
10. Berry and Allen, 67.
11. Fischer, *Albion's Seed*, 502–3.
12. Philadelphia Monthly Meeting, Births.
13. Jean R. Soderlund, et al. *William Penn and the Founding of Pennsylvania 1680–1684* . . . (Philadelphia, 1983), 197.
14. Middletown [Bucks Co.] Monthly Meeting, Minutes.
15. Ibid.
16. Goshen [Chester Co.] Monthly Meeting, Births.
17. Uwchlan [Chester Co.] Monthly Meeting, Births; hereafter cited as Uwchlan Births.
18. Uwchlan [Chester Co.] Monthly Meeting, Minutes; hereafter cited as Uwchlan Minutes.
19. Ibid.
20. Uwchlan Births.
21. Nottingham [Chester Co.] Monthly Meeting, Births.
22. New Garden [Chester Co.] Monthly Meeting, Births.
23. Uwchlan Minutes.
24. Ibid.
25. William Wade Hinshaw, *Encyclopedia of American Quaker Genealogy* . . . (Baltimore, 1969), 2: 428.
26. Abstracts of Philadelphia County Wills.

Chapter 8: Evaluating the Evidence, pages 83–96

1. Glatfelter, 2: 151.
2. Ibid., 2: 150.
3. Hinke, *Coetus*, 4.
4. Glatfelter, 2: 189–97.
5. Tappart and Doberstein, 1: 366.
6. Trinity [Episcopal] Church, Oxford Twp. [Philadelphia Co.], Baptisms.

7. Tappart and Doberstein, 1: 570.

8. St. Michael's and Zion.

9. Ibid.

10. Gloria Dei.

11. St. Michael's and Zion.

12. Scots Presbyterian Church, Philadelphia, Baptisms; hereafter cited as Scots Presbytrian.

13. Abington [Montgomery Co.] Presbyterian Church, Baptisms.

14. Ibid.

15. Hinke, *Coetus*, 128.

16. St. Michael's and Zion.

17. Tinicum Presbyterian.

18. Photostat copy and translation of a baptismal certificate for a child of John Nicholaus and Anna Steiger, dated 1688.

19. Second Presbyterian Church, Philadelphia, Baptisms.

20. First Reformed Church, Philadelphia, Baptisms.

Chapter 9: About Baptismal Registers, pages 97–114

1. Louis C. Washburn, *Christ Church, Philadelphia* (Philadelphia, 1925), 19.

2. Glatfelter, 2: 153

3. Tappart and Doberstein, 1: 170.

4. Glatfelter, 1: 327.

5. Klett, *Colonial Pennsylvania*, 89–97.

6. Tappart and Doberstein, 2: 409.

7. William N. Schwarze and Ralf Ridgway Hillman, trans., *The Dansbury Diaries: Moravian Travel Diaries, 1748–1755* . . . (Camden, Me., 1994), 55–56.

8. Klett, *Colonial Pennsylvania*, 97–101.

9. Tappart and Doberstein, 2: 181.

10. Glatfelter, 2: 148.

11. Klett, *Colonial Pennsylvania*, 230.

12. Morton L. Montgomery, *History of Berks County, Pa.* (Philadelphia, 1886), 783.

13. Presbytery Minutes of Donegal, Lancaster Co.

14. Glatfelter, 2: 460.

15. Christ [Episcopal] Church, Philadelphia, Baptisms.

16. Washburn, 20.

17. Philadelphia Monthly Meeting, Abstract of Minutes.

18. Philadelphia Monthly Meeting, Births.

19. Ibid.

20. Abington [Montgomery Co.] Monthly Meeting, Minutes.

21. Ibid.

22. Chester [Chester Co.] Monthly Meeting, Births.

23. Glatfelter, 1: 413.

24. Hinke, *Coetus*, 77. One of the books that came from Holland was used as a personal register by Rev. John Waldschmidt, and baptisms can be found in that register for four Reformed congregations that he served in Lancaster Co.: Cocalico, Muddy Creek, Reyers, and Seltenreich.

25. Andrews, personal register.

26. First Presbyterian Church, Philadelphia, Baptisms.

27. Ibid.

28. Ibid.
29. Second Presbyterian Church, Philadelphia, Baptisms.
30. Second Presbyterian, Philadelphia, Session Records.
31. A private personal baptismal record kept by Rev. Gilbert Tennent, if it exists, is not held in the collections of the Presbyterian Historical Society in Philadelphia. It is possible that Rev. Tennent's record has been lost, or perhaps it can be found in another repository.
32. Glatfelter, 1: 84.
33. Andrews, personal register.
34. Ibid.
35. Glatfelter, 2: 402.

Chapter 10: Activities Related to Baptism, pages 115–124

1. Blunt, 408.
2. Tappart and Doberstein, 2: 146.
3. Ibid., 1: 93.
4. Ibid., 1: 96.
5. Carl Theo. Eben, *Gottlieb Mittelberger's Journey To Pennsylvania* . . . (Philadelphia, 1898), 68–69.
6. Gloria Dei.
7. Ibid.
8. Ibid.
9. Tappart and Doberstein, 2: 524.
10. Ibid., 1: 709.
11. Frederick S. Weiser and Howell J. Heaney, *The Pennsylvania German Fraktur of The Free Library of Philadelphia* . . . (Breinigsville, Pa., 1976), 1: xxii.
12. Eben, 61.
13. Tappart and Doberstein, 1: 84.
14. Hinke, *Coetus*, 44.
15. Tappart and Doberstein, 2: 520.
16. Ibid., 2: 495.
17. Glatfelter, 2: 246.
18. Tappart and Doberstein, 1: 101.
19. Frederick S. Weiser, "The Concept of Baptism Among Colonial Pennsylvania German Lutheran and Reformed Church People," *Essays and Reports* 4 (1970): 9.
20. Tappart and Doberstein, 1: 617.
21. Ibid., 1: 696.
22. Ibid., 1: 500.
23. St. Michael's and Zion.
24. German Reformed Congregation, Germantown (Philadelphia), Births; hereafter cited as Germantown Reformed.
25. Tappart and Doberstein, 1: 656.
26. Glatfelter, 2: 250.
27. Old St. Joseph's Catholic.
28. Germantown Reformed.
29. Charles R. Hildeburn, *Baptisms and Burials* . . . *Christ Church, Philadelphia* (Baltimore, 1982), 5.
30. Old St. Joseph's Catholic.

Chapter 11: Record Problems, pages 125–134

1. St. Michael's Lutheran Church, Germantown, Births.
2. Ibid.
3. Germantown Reformed.
4. *History of the Jerusalem Lutheran and Reformed Church of Western Salisbury, Lehigh Co., Penna.* . . . (Allentown, Pa., 1911), 120; hereafter cited as *Jerusalem Lutheran and Reformed.*
5. *Pennsylvania German Church Records, Volume 3: The Tohickon Lutheran Church,* 3: 363–64.
6. Ibid., 43–44.
7. Philadelphia Second Presbyterian, Baptisms.
8. *Goshenhoppen Registers,* 14.
9. *Jerusalem Lutheran and Reformed,* 120–21.
10. William J. Hinke, "Church Record of Zion Reformed Church, Allentown . . . , 1765–1820" (Allentown, 1938), 1: 1.
11. "Records of the Reformed Congregation in Lower Saucon Township" (undated TS): 20, 23, 28, 36, 40.
12. Weiser and Heaney, 2: plate 301.
13. Scots Presbyterian.
14. *Goshenhoppen Register,* 26, 33.
15. Old St. Joseph's Catholic.
16. St. Michael's and Zion.
17. Tappart and Doberstein, 2: 562.
18. St. Michael's and Zion.
19. Gloria Dei.
20. Old St. Joseph's Catholic.
21. Glatfelter, 1: 5; 2: 146, 2: 194, 2: 196–97, 2: 202.
22. Ibid., 1: 24, 1: 152.
23. Ibid., 2: 148.

Chapter 12: Additional Considerations, pages 141–139

1. Guy Soulliard Klett, ed., *Journals of Charles Beatty 1762–1769,* (University Park, Pa., 1962), 50.
2. Ibid.
3. Fagg's Manor Presbyterian Church, Cochranville [Chester Co.], Session Minutes.
4. Gloria Dei.
5. Tappart and Doberstein, 1: 122.
6. Ibid., 2: 122–48.
7. Fries, 1: 266.
8. Tappart and Doberstein, 1: 615.
9. St. Michael's and Zion.
10. Eben, 69.
11. Tappart and Doberstein, 1: 310.
12. Ibid., 1: 236.

Bibliography

Original Records

Original records are listed below, by location, according to the repository used for citations in the preceding "Notes" section. These records take a variety of forms—original documents, photocopies of original documents, compiled lists, microfilm, etc. Because some of these church records exist in more than one medium and/or under more than one title, distinctions among the various forms are not noted.

Significant inconsistencies persist within and between source materials regarding the span of dates covered; therefore, inclusive dates of original records used are not listed. Researchers should check with each repository for the availability of information about specific church records for specific years.

Many of the materials listed are unpaginated or contain page numbers assigned by an after-the-fact compiler; additionally, a comparison of otherwise duplicate records sometimes reveals apparent pagination inconsistency. To avoid posible confusion, no page numbers have been included in the "Notes" section for citations taken from original records.

Although researchers will find that many of these church documents have been reproduced by the Family History Library, no claim is made that all listed birth/baptismal records are available through FHL.

Friends Historical Library, Swarthmore College, Swarthmore, Pa.

Bucks Co.: Middletown Monthly Meeting, Minutes.
Chester Co.: Chester Monthly Meeting, Births.
Chester Co.: Fallowfield Monthly Meeting, Births.
Chester Co.: Goshen Monthly Meeting, Births.
Chester Co.: Kennett Monthly Meeting, Minutes.
Chester Co.: Kennett Monthly Meeting, Births.
Chester Co.: New Garden Monthly Meeting, Births.
Chester Co.: Nottingham Monthly Meeting, Births.
Chester Co.: Uwchlan Monthly Meeting, Births.

Chester Co.: Uwchlan Monthly Meeting, Minutes.
Montgomery Co.: Abington Monthly Meeting, Births.
Montgomery Co.: Abington Monthly Meeting, Minutes.
Philadelphia: Philadelphia Monthly Meeting, Births.

Collections of the Genealogical Society of Pennsylvania,
Historical Society of Pennsylvania Library, Philadelphia, Pa.

Chester Co.: Chester County Friends Monthly Meeting Records.
Germantown (Philadelphia): German Reformed Congregation, Baptisms.
Germantown (Philadelphia): St. Michael's Lutheran Church, Baptisms.
Lehigh Co.: Salisbury (now Emmaus), Birth and Baptismal Register for the [Moravian] Congrega-
    tion, Baptisms.
Montgomery Co.: Abington Monthly Meeting, Abstract of Records of Marriages, Births, and
    Deaths.
Montgomery Co.: Abington Presbyterian Church, Baptisms.
Philadelphia: Abstracts of Philadelphia County Wills.
Philadelphia: Christ [Episcopal] Church, Baptisms.
Philadelphia: First Baptist Church, Baptisms.
Philadelphia: First Presbyterian Church, Baptisms.
Philadelphia: First Reformed Church, Baptisms.
Philadelphia: Gloria Dei (Old Swedes) Lutheran Church, Baptisms.
Philadelphia: Old St. Joseph's Catholic Church, Baptisms.
Philadelphia: Philadelphia Monthly Meeting, Abstract of Minutes.
Philadelphia: Philadelphia Monthly Meeting, Births.
Philadelphia: Scots Presbyterian Church, Baptisms.
Philadelphia: Second Presbyterian Church, Baptisms.
Philadelphia: St. George's Methodist Episcopal Church, Baptisms.
Philadelphia: St. Michael's and Zion Evangelical Lutheran Church, Baptisms.
Philadelphia: St. Paul's [Episcopal] Church, Baptisms.
Philadelphia Co.: Pennypack Baptist Church, Baptisms.
Philadelphia Co.: Trinity [Episcopal] Church, Oxford Twp., Baptisms.

Presbyterian Historical Society Library, Philadelphia, Pa.

Bucks Co.: Newtown Presbyterian Church, Baptisms.
Bucks Co.: Tinicum Presbyterian Church, Red Hill, Congregational Records.
Chester Co.: Carmichael, Rev. John, personal register.
Chester Co.: Fagg's Manor Presbyterian Church, Cochranville, Session Minutes.
Chester Co.: Forks of the Brandywine Presbyterian Church, Session Records.
Chester Co.: Presbyterian Church, Oxford, Session Minutes.
Lancaster Co.: Presbytery Minutes of Donegal, Baptisms.
Montgomery Co.: Abington Presbyterian Church, Baptisms.
Montgomery Co.: Abington Presbyterian Church, Session Register.
Philadelphia: Andrews, Rev. Jedediah, personal register.
Philadelphia: First Presbyterian Church, Baptisms.
Philadelphia: Marshall, Rev. William, personal register.
Philadelphia: Second Presbyterian Church, Baptisms.
Philadelphia: Second Presbyterian Church, Minutes of the Congregation.
Philadelphia: Second Presbyterian Church, Session Records.
Philadelphia: Scots Presbyterian Church, Baptisms.

Unpublished Works

Archives of the United Church of Christ, Franklin and Marshall College, Lancaster, Pa.

Schellhase, Richard T. "The Reformed Church in the United States." Lancaster, Pa., n.d.

Easton Area Public Library, Easton, Pa.

"Records of the Reformed Congregation in Lower Saucon Township" (undated typescript).

Lehigh County Historical Society Library, Allentown, Pa.

Hinke, William J. "Church Record of Zion Reformed Church, Allentown, Lehigh County, Volume 1, 1765–1820." Allentown, Pa., 1938.
Seckel, Clarence E., comp., "Records of St. Paul's Lutheran and Reformed Church (Blue Church) in Upper Saucon Township, Lehigh County, Pennsylvania, 1748–1892," 2 vols. Bethlehem, Pa., 1939.

Reeves Library, Moravian College, Bethlehem, Pa.

Helmich, Carl John. "Infant Baptism in the Moravian Church: A Study of Doctrine and Liturgy." Thesis, Bethlehem, Pa., 1957.

Published Works

Aries, Philippe, and Georges Duby. *A History of Private Life. Volume III: Passions of the Renaissance.* Cambridge, Mass.: Harvard Univ. Press, 1989.
Berry, Ellen Thomas, and David Allen. *Our Quaker Ancestors.* Baltimore, Md.: Genealogical Publishing Co., 1987.
Blunt, John Henry, ed. *The Annotated Book of Common Prayer, Being an Historical, Ritual, and Theological Commentary on the Devotional System of the Church of England.* New York, N.Y.: E. P. Dutton and Co., 1903.
Bodensieck, Julius, ed. *The Encyclopedia of the Lutheran Church.* 3 vols. Minneapolis, Minn.: Augsburg Publishing House, 1965.
Borduin, Menno. *Form of Baptism Explained.* Grand Rapids, Mich.: Zondervan Publishing House, 1935.
The Book of Order of the Moravian Church in America (Unitas Fratrum), Northern Province. Bethlehem, Pa., 1911.
Braithwaite, William C. *The Beginnings of Quakerism.* London: MacMillan and Co., Ltd., 1912.
Bucke, Emory Stevens, ed. *The History of American Methodism.* 3 vols. New York, N.Y.: Abingdon Press, 1964.
Cameron, Euan. *The European Reformation.* Oxford, England: Clarendon Press, 1991.
Cathcart, William, ed. *The Baptist Encyclopedia: A Dictionary of the Doctrines, Ordinances, Usages, Confessions of Faith, Sufferings, Labors and Successes, and of the General History of the Baptist Denomination in All Lands, with Numerous Biographical Sketches of Distinguished American and Foreign Baptists and a Supplement.* Philadelphia, Pa.: Louis H. Everts, 1881.

Collections of the New York Genealogical and Biographical Society. New York, N.Y.: New York Genealogical and Biographical Society, 1928. Volume 8: "Presbyterian Church Records, Newtown (now Elmhurst), Long Island, NY."; "The Reformed Dutch Church Records and the Presbyterian Church Records at Smithfield, Pa."; " Clove Dutch Reformed Church Records of Clove Valley, Wantage, N.J."

A Concise Historical Account of the Present Constitution of the Protestant Church of the United Brethren Adhering to the Confession of Augsburg. Manchester, England: n.p., 1815.

Constitution and Discipline of the German Reformed Church in the United States of America, Approved by the Classes and Adopted 1828. Chambersburg, Pa.: n.p., 1828.

The Constitution of the Presbyterian Church (U.S.A.). Part II: Book of Order. Louisville, Ky.: Office of the General Assembly, 1992.

Cooper, Wilmer A. *A Living Faith: An Historical Study of Quaker Beliefs.* Richmond, Ind.: Friends United Press, 1990.

Doctrines and Discipline of the Methodist Church. New York, N.Y.: Methodist Publishing House, 1939.

Durant, Will. *The Story of Civilization, Part IV. The Age of Faith: A History of Medieval Civilization—Christian, Islamic, and Judaic—from Constantine to Dante, A.D. 325–1300.* New York, N.Y.: Simon and Schuster, 1950.

————. *The Story of Civilization, Part VI. The Reformation: A History of European Civilization from Wyclif to Calvin, 1300–1564.* New York, N.Y.: Simon and Schuster, 1957.

Durnbaugh, Donald F., ed. *The Brethren Encyclopedia.* Philadelphia:Pa. Brethren Encyclopedia, Inc., 1983.

————. *Brethren Beginnings: The Origin of the Church of the Brethren in Early Eighteenth Century Europe.* Philadelphia, Pa.: Brethren Encyclopedia, Inc., 1992.

————. *Church of the Brethren, Yesterday and Today.* Elgin, Ill.: Brethren Press,1988.

————. *European Origins of the Brethren.* Elgin, Ill.: Brethren Press, 1958.

Earnest, Corinne Pattie, and Beverly Repass Hoch. *The Genealogists' Guide to Fraktur for Genealogists Researching German-American Families.* Albuquerque, N.M.: Russell D. Earnest Assoc., 1990.

Eben, Carl Theo., trans. *Gottlieb Mittleberger's Journey to Pennsylvania in the Year 1750 and Return to Germany in the Year 1754, Containing Not Only a Description of the Country According to Its Present Condition, But Also a Detailed Account of the Sad and Unfortunate Circumstances of Most of the Germans That Have Emigrated, Or Are Emigrants to That Country.* Philadelphia, Pa.: privately printed, 1898.

Enciclopedia Cattolica. Frienze (Florence), Italy: L'enciclopedia Cattolica e per Il Libro Cattolico, Citta Del Vaticano (Vatican City), 1949.

Encyclopedia of Southern Baptists. Nashville, Tenn.: Broadman Press, 1958.

Eshleman, H. Frank. *Historic Background and Annals of the Swiss and German Pioneer Settlers of Southeastern Pennsylvania, and of Their Remote Ancestors, From the Middle of the Dark Ages, Down to the Time of the Revolutionary War.* Lancaster, Pa.: n.p., 1917.

Fields, S. Helen. *Register of Marriages and Baptisms Performed by Rev. John Cuthbertson Covenanter, Minister, 1751–1791, With Index to Locations and Persons Visited.* Baltimore, Md.: Genealogical Publishing Co., Inc., 1983.

Fischer, David Hackett. *Albion's Seed: Four British Folkways in America.* New York, N.Y.: Oxford Univ. Press, 1989.

Fischer, Robert H., trans. *The Large Catechism of Martin Luther.* Philadelphia, Pa.: Muhlenberg Press, 1959.

Fries, Adelaide L., trans. *Records of the Moravians in North Carolina.* 11 vols. Raleigh, N.C.: State Department of Archives and History, 1968 reprint.

Gardner, David E. and Frank Smith. *Volume 1: Genealogical Research in England and Wales.* Salt Lake City, Utah: Bookcraft Publishers, 1956.

Gear, Felix B. *Our Presbyterian Belief.* Atlanta, Ga.: John Knox Press, 1980.

Glatfelter, Charles H. *Pastors and People: German Lutheran and Reformed Churches in the Pennsylvania Field, 1717–1793, Volume I: Pastors and Congregations.* Breinigsville, Pa.: Pennsylvania German Society, 1980.

———— . *Pastors and People: German Lutheran and Reformed Churches in the Pennsylvania Field, 1717–1793, Volume II: The History.* Breinigsville, Pa.: Pennsylvania German Society, 1981.

The Goshenhoppen Registers, 1741–1819: Registers of Baptisms, Marriages, and Deaths of the Catholic Mission at Goshenhoppen (Bally), Washington Township, Berks County, Pennsylvania. Baltimore, Md.: Genealogical Publishing Co., Inc., 1984. (Reprinted from records of the American Catholic Historical Society of Philadelphia.)

Hamilton, Kenneth G., trans. *The Bethlehem Diary, Volume I: 1742–1744.* Bethlehem, Pa.: Archives of the Moravian Church, 1971.

Hammonds, Kenneth A. *Historical Directory of Presbyterian Churches and Presbyteries of Greater Philadelphia.* Philadelphia, Pa.: Presbyterian Historical Society, 1993.

Hanawalt, Barbara A. *Growing Up in Medieval London: The Experience of Childhood in History.* New York, N.Y.: Oxford Univ. Press, 1993.

Harmon, Nolan B. *The Encyclopedia of World Methodism.* Nashville, Tenn.: United Methodist Publishing House, 1974.

The Heidelberg Catechism, Or Instruction in Christian Doctrine As It Is Conducted by the Churches and Schools of the Palatinate and Elsewhere. Chambersburg, Pa.: n.p., 1854.

The Heidelberg Catechism Together with the Constitution and Discipline of the German Reformed Church in the United States of America. Chambersburg, Pa.: n.p., 1841.

Hey, David. *The Oxford Guide to Family History.* New York, N.Y.: Oxford Univ. Press, 1993.

Hildeburn, Charles R. *Baptisms and Burials from the Records of Christ Church, Philadelphia, 1709–1760.* Baltimore, Md.: Genealogical Publishing Co., 1982.

Hinke, William J. *Early History of the Reformed Church in Pennsylvania.* Reading, Pa.: n.p., 1906.

———— . *Minutes and Letters of the Coetus of the German Reformed Congregations in Pennsylvania, 1747–1792, Together with Three Preliminary Reports of Rev. John Philip Boehm, 1734–1744.* Philadelphia, Pa.: Reformed Church Publishing Board, 1903.

Hinshaw, William Wade. *Encyclopedia of American Quaker Genealogy. Volume II: Containing Every Item of Genealogical Value Found in All Records and Minutes (Known To Be in Existence) of Four of the Oldest Monthly Meetings Which Ever Belonged to the Philadelphia Yearly Meeting of Friends.* Baltimore, Md.: Genealogical Publishing Co., 1969.

History of Jerusalem Lutheran and Reformed Church of Western Salisbury, Lehigh Co., Penna., With Complete Records of All Members of Both Congregations: Baptisms, Confirmations, Marriages, Burials. Allentown, Pa.: H. Ray Haas and Co., 1911.

Holborn, Hajo. *A History of Modern Germany: The Reformation.* Princeton, N.J.: Princeton Univ. Press, 1959.

The Holy Bible. Camden, N.J.: Thomas Nelson and Sons, 1959. (Revised Standard Edition.)

Ives, J. Moss. *The Ark and the Dove: The Beginnings of Civil and Religious Liberties in America.* New York, N.Y.: Longmans Green and Co., 1936.

Jeremias, Joachim. *The Origins of Infant Baptism: A Further Study in Reply to Kurt Aland.* Naperville, Ill.: Alec R. Allenson, n.d.

Johnson, Paul. *A History of Christianity.* New York, N.Y.: Atheneum, 1977.

Kirlin, Joseph L. *Catholicity in Philadelphia, From the Earliest Missionaries Down to the Present Time.* Philadelphia, Pa.: John Jos. McVey, 1909.

Klees, Frederic. *The Pennsylvania Dutch.* New York, N.Y.: MacMillan, 1950.

Klett, Guy Soulliard. *Minutes of the Presbyterian Church in America, 1706–1788.* Philadelphia, Pa.: Presbyterian Historical Society, 1976.

———— , ed. *Journals of Charles Beatty, 1762–1769.* University Park, Pa.: Pennsylvania State Univ. Press, 1962.

———— . *Presbyterians in Colonial Pennsylvania.* Philadelphia, Pa.: Univ. of Pennsylvania Press, 1937.

Levering, Joseph Mortimer. *A History of Bethlehem, Pennsylvania, 1741–1892, With Some Accounts of Its Founders and Their Early Activity in America.* Bethlehem, Pa.: Times Publishing Co., 1903.

Lynch, Joseph H. *Godparents and Kinship in Early Medieval Europe.* Princeton, N.J.: Princeton Univ. Press, 1986.

Lundeen, Joel, W., ed. *Luther's Works.* 55 vols. Philadelphia, Pa.: Frontier Press, 1986.

McBeth, H. Leon, *The Baptist Heritage*. Nashville, Tenn.: Broadman Press, 1987.

McKim, Donald K., ed. *Encyclopedia of the Reformed Faith*. Louisville, Ky.: John Knox Press, 1992.

The Mennonite Encyclopedia: A Comprehensive Reference Work on the Anabaptist-Mennonite Movement. 3 vols. Scottdale, Pa.: Mennonite Brethren Publishing House, 1955.

Montgomery, Morton, L. *History of Berks County, Pa*. Philadelphia, Pa.: Everts, Peck and Richards, 1886.

Moorman, John R. H. *A History of the Church of England*. London: A. and C. Black, 1953.

New Catholic Encyclopedia. 18 vols. Washington, D.C.: Catholic Univ. of America, 1980.

Pennsylvania German Church Records of Births, Baptisms, Marriages, Burials, etc., From the Pennsylvania German Society Proceedings and Addresses. 3 vols. Baltimore, Md.: Genealogical Publishing Co., Inc., 1983.

Phillimore, Sir Robert. *The Ecclesiastical Law of the Church of England*. London: Sweet and Maxwell, Ltd., 1895.

Pritchard, Robert W. *A History of the Episcopal Church*. Harrisburg, Pa.: Morehouse Publishing Co., 1991.

Rubincam, Milton, ed. Volume 1: *Genealogical Research: Methods and Sources*. Washington, DC: American Society of Genealogists, 1980.

Sarpi, Paolo, *The History of the Council of Trent*. London: J. Madcock, 1676.

Schwarz, Ralph Grayson. *Bethlehem on the Lehigh*. Bethlehem, Pa.: Bethlehem Area Foundation, 1991.

Schwarze, William N., and Ralf Ridgway Hillman, trans. *The Dansbury Diaries: Moravian Travel Diaries, 1748–1755, of the Reverend Sven Roseen and Others in the Area of Dansbury, Now Stroudsburg, Pa*. Camden, Me.: Picton Press, 1994.

Scott, Stephen. *The Amish Wedding and Other Special Occasions of the Old Order Communities*. Intercourse, Pa.: Good Books, 1988.

Smaby, Beverly Prior. *The Transformation of Moravian Bethlehem from Communal Mission to Family Economy*. Philadelphia, Pa.: Univ. of Pennsylvania Press, 1988.

Snyder, Martin P. *City of Independence: Views of Philadelphia Before 1800*. New York, N.Y.: Praeger Publishers, 1975.

Soderlund, Jean R., et al. *William Penn and the Founding of Pennsylvania, 1680–1684: A Documentary History*. Philadelphia, Pa.: Univ. of Pennsylvania Press, 1983.

Sprague, William B. *Annals of the American Pulpit*. 9 vols. New York: Arno Press and the New York Times, 1969.

The Statutes of the Realm, Printed by Command of His Majesty King George the Third, From Original Records and Authentic Manuscript. 9 vols. Buffalo, N.Y.: William S. Hein and Co., 1993.

Tappart, Theodore G., and John W. Doberstein, trans. *The Journals of Henry Melchior Muhlenberg*. 3 vols. Philadelphia, Pa.: Muhlenberg Press, 1942.

Washburn, Louis C. *Christ Church, Philadelphia*. Philadelphia, Pa.: Macrae Smith Co., 1925.

Weiser, Frederick S. "The Concept of Baptism Among Colonial Pennsylvania German Lutheran and Reformed Church People," *Essays and Reports* 4 (1970): 1–45.

Weiser, Frederick S., and Howell J. Heaney. *The Pennsylvania German Fraktur of the Free Library of Philadelphia: An Illustrated Catalogue*. 2 vols. Breinigsville, Pa.: Pennsylvania German Society, 1976.

Woodroofe, Helen Hutchison. "A Chronological List of Philadelphia Churches and Cemeteries, 1642–1790," *Pennsylvania Genealogical Magazine* 30 (1978): 150–72.

Woodroofe, Helen Hutchison. "Baptisms from the Church Book of the German Reformed Church of Philadelphia, by Reverend Friedrich S. Rothenbueler, 1762–1763," *Pennsylvania Genealogical Magazine* 35 (1987): 9–16.

Index

A

Abington Monthly Meeting, Montgomery Co., Pa., 105–6
Abington Presbyterian Church, Montgomery Co., Pa., 48, 56, 90
Adams Co., Pa., 84
African-American, 89–92, 118
agape, 67
Allentown, Lehigh Co., Pa., 128
Allison, Doct., 110
Alsentz, Rev. George, 121
America, 11, 33, 63, 101, 143
American, Native (*see* Indian, American)
American Colonies, 6–7, 33, 35–37, 41, 56, 66, 101
American Revolution, 35–36, 42–43, 88, 114, 126
Amish Mennonite Church (*see* denomination, Amish Mennonite)
Ammann, Bishop Jakob, 63, 81
Amsterdam, 61
Anabaptist (*see* denomination, Anabaptist)
Anabaptist, Swiss, 63
Andrews, Rev. Jedidiah, 50, 109, 112–13
Anglican Church (*see* denomination, Anglican)
Arnold, Gottfried, 67
Asbury, Bishop Francis, 42, 82
Asky, Archibald, 23
aspersion, 15, 18, 32, 37, 117
Austria, 60–61

B

Backhouse, Rev. Richard, 102
Bacon Ridge, Somerset Co., N.J., 132
Bader
    Catharine, 29
    Johannes, 29
    Mary, 29
Bally, Berks Co., Pa., 7
Baltimore, Lord, 7
Baltimore, Maryland, 42
baptism
    adult, 1, 12, 14–16, 31, 52, 59, 61, 63, 67, 83, 93–94, 103, 109, 137–38
    anonymous, 136
    believer, 59–60, 63
    conditional, 13, 17–18, 22, 28, 32, 42, 47, 54
    emergency, 1, 13, 17, 21, 28, 32, 42, 47, 54, 86, 89, 93, 115, 121–22, 137–39
    English, 86, 91
    infant, 11, 15–22, 27, 29–33, 35–37, 39–40, 42–43, 46–47, 50, 52–53, 55, 59–61, 64–65, 67, 72, 78, 83–84, 86–95, 100, 108, 115, 118–23, 131, 134, 137–38
    initiation rite of, 13–14, 18, 28, 31, 45, 61, 63–64, 94
    lay, 17, 21, 32, 86, 137–38
    of the Holy Spirit, 15, 55, 67, 69
    openness, 21, 32, 39, 86, 89–90, 92
    ordinance of, 48, 50
    private, 22, 31–32, 37, 46, 88, 93, 117
    public, 31–32
    unrecorded, 98, 119, 121, 135, 137
Baptist Church (*see* denomination, Baptist)

156

Baptist
  English, 6
  Keithian, 66
Barnard
  Ann, 76
  Hannah, 76
  John, 76
  Joshua, 76
  Sarah, 76
  Thomas, 76
Bayard, John, 111
Beatty, Rev. Charles, 135–36, 139
Beissel, Conrad, 59
Bender
  Elisabeth, 138
  Johannes, 138
Berks Co., Pa., 7, 21, 28, 68, 84, 98, 102, 112,
  127, 131
Bermuda, 35
Bethabara, North Carolina, 137
Bethlehem, Northampton Co., Pa., 38, 100
birth
  illegitimate, 22–23, 29, 52, 78, 82
  questionable, 22–23, 52, 78
Bischof, Peter, 22
bishop, 8, 10, 15, 17, 24, 32–33, 36, 45, 63–64
Bishop of London, 98
Bisschof
  Charlotte, 22
  Mary, 22
  Pete, 22
  Peter, 22
  Philip James, 22
Boarshead, London, 103
Boehm, Rev. John Philip, 84, 108
Bohemia, 93
Bohler
  Ludwig Friedrich, 41
  Maria Christ., 41
Book of Common Prayer, 10, 31–32, 115
Boone, George, 105
Boyd
  Alexander, 130
  James, 130
  Jane, 130
BrandywineBaptist Church, Chester Co., Pa.,
  66
Brandywine Presbyterian Church, Chester
  Co., Pa., 47, 49
Bratton
  Andrew, 135
  Mifflin Co., Pa., 135
Braunschweig, North Carolina, 137

Brethren
  Baptist 67–68 (see also denomination,
    Dunkard/Brethren)
  Moravian, 37, 41, 100 (see also denomination,
    Moravian
  Swiss, 60–61, 63 (see also denomination,
    Mennonite)
Bridges
  John, 117
  Mary, 117
Brinck
  Arie, 57
  Lambart, 57
Broadhead, Daniel, 57
Brosius
  Henry, 78
  Mary, 78
Bruch family, 133
Brunner
  Andreas, 129–30
  Anna Margaretha, 129
  Christina, 129–30
  Heinrich, 129
  Magdalena, 129
  Maria Eva, 130
Brunnholtz, Rev. Peter, 29–31
Bucher, Rev. John Conrad, 112, 132
Bucks Co., Pa., 48–51, 55–56, 66, 73, 84–85,
  101, 109, 121, 126, 130–33, 135
Bullinger, Heinrich, 51
Burlington Co., N.J., 132

C

Calvin, John, 45–47, 51, 54, 56, 64–65, 69, 80
Canada, 35–36
Cape Fear River, North Carolina, 137
Carmichael, Rev. John, 49
Carroll, Bishop John, 24, 82
Catechism, Heidelerg, 51–52
Catholic Church (see denomination, Catholic)
certificate
  baptismal, 54, 118
  birth, 71–72
  membership, 47, 53
Charles I, 9
Chester Co., Pa., 47–50, 66, 68, 75, 78, 84–85,
  103, 109, 131–32, 136
Chester Monthly Meeting, Chester Co., Pa.,
  105, 107
Chichester, 103
chrism, 18, 27

Martin
  Sarah, 75–76
  Thomas, 75–76
Maryland, 7–8, 24, 35, 84, 100
Meeting
  Monthly, 70–75, 77–78, 103, 105–7
  Preparative, 70, 75
  Quarterly, 70–71, 75
  Yearly, 70
Meidung, 63
Melanchthon, Philip, 51
Mennonite Church (*see* denomination,
    Mennonite
Methodist Church (*see* denomination,
    Methodist)
Meurer, Philip, 40
Middletown Monthly Meeting, Bucks Co.,
    Pa., 73
midwife, 17–18, 21, 71–72, 93, 115, 119, 138–39
Mifflin Co., Pa., 135
Milhouse, Thomas, Jr., 75
Millbach Reformed Church, Lebanon Co.,
    Pa., 126
Milleberry, Rev., 90
minister
  Anglican, 5, 10, 32–33, 35, 41–42, 83, 85–86,
    98, 101–2, 115, 132, 137
  Baptist, 10, 66, 92
  Catholic, 6–8, 16–18, 20–23, 76, 85, 89, 93, 102,
    121–22, 124, 131–32, 138
  Congregationalist, 10
  Dunkard/Brethren, 92
  Dutch Reformed, 56, 85, 90
  English, 7, 10, 137
  Episcopal, 35, 43, 73, 86
  German Jesuit, 7–8
  German Reformed, 52
  German Lutheran, 73, 108, 118, 121
  itinerant/unordained, 42, 84, 98–100, 118
  Jesuit, 85, 93
  Low Dutch Reformed, 56
  Lutheran, 28–30, 77, 84–86, 88, 91–92, 100,
    108, 112, 114–16, 119–20, 126, 128, 132,
    136, 138
  Mennonite, 92, 99
  Methodist, 42
  Moravian, 11, 37, 39–41, 85, 137
  ordained, 45, 99, 101
  Presbyterian, 10, 22, 47–50, 56, 73, 90, 94,
    100–2, 109–13, 130, 132, 135–36
  Reformed, 52–55, 84–85, 91, 94, 98, 100–2,
    108–9, 112, 114, 119, 121–22, 126–128,
    130, 132

minister (continued)
  Swedish Lutheran, 28, 88, 102, 117–18, 132,
    136
Mischler, Peter, 99
Mittelberger, Gottlieb, 116, 118, 138
Mohr family, 133
Mohr, Maria Eva, 130
Monroe Co., Pa., 55–57, 84
Montgomery, 103
Montgomery Co., Pa., 26, 33, 44, 48, 56, 84,
    90, 105, 108–9, 119, 127, 131–32
Moravia, 36
Moravian Church (*see* denomination,
    Moravian)
Muddy Creek, Lancaster Co., Pa., 147
Muhlenberg, Rev. Henry Melchior, 26, 28–29,
    31, 33, 77, 82, 85–86, 98–99, 101, 108,
    112, 114–16, 118–21, 131, 136–37, 139
Munzer, Thomas, 59
Murray
  Elizabeth, 22
  Hugh, 22
  Margaret, 22
Myrc, John, 17

N

naming system
  fixed, 57
  patronymic, 56–57
Native American (*see* Indian, American)
Nantmeal Preparative Meeting, Chester Co.,
    Pa., 75
Nedermark, Jane, 29
Neil
  Daniel, 48
  Tilyer, 48
Neshaminy Presbyterian Church, Bucks Co.,
    Pa., 135
Neshaminy, Bucks Co., Pa., 85, 130
Netherlands (*see* Holland)
Neu, Joh. Andreas, 100
New England, 9, 66
New Garden Monthly Meeting, Chester Co.,
    Pa., 76
New Goshenhoppen Reformed Church,
    Montgomery Co., Pa., 127
New Hanover Lutheran Church,
    Montgomery Co., Pa., 26, 108, 119
New Hanover, Montgomery Co., Pa., 132
New Jersey, 66, 103, 121–22, 131–32
New Providence, Montgomery Co., Pa., 33
New York, 35, 55–57

Also by John T. Humphrey

PENNSYLVANIA BIRTHS SERIES

Bucks County, 1682–1800..over 12,200 recorded births

Chester County, 1682–1800..over 9,400 recorded births

Delaware County, 1682–1800...over 4,500 recorded births

Lebanon County, 1714–1800..over 7,500 recorded births

Lehigh Couty, 1734–1800...over 11,000 recorded births

Montgomery County, 1682–1800...over 18,200 recorded births

Northampton County, 1733–1800...over 7,700 recorded births

Philadelphia County, 1644–1765..over 17,600 recorded births

Philadelphia County, 1766–1780..over 17,000 recorded births

FAMILY HISTORIES

Early Families of Northampton County, Pennsylvania, Vol. 1: Frack/Seyfried

Early Families of Northampton County, Pennsylvania, Vol. 2: Repsher/Dietrich